A GUIDE TO PHILIPPIANS

TEF Study Guides

This SPCK series was originally sponsored and subsidized by the Theological Education Fund of the WCC in response to requests from Africa, Asia, the Caribbean, and the Pacific. The books are prepared by and in consultation with theological tutors from all over the world, but have from the outset been as widely used by students and parish groups in the West as by those for whom English may be a second language. More advanced titles in the list are marked (A).

General Editors: Daphne Terry and Nicholas Beddow

ALREADY PUBLISHED

1. A Guide to the Parables
2. A Guide to St Mark's Gospel
3. A Guide to Genesis
4. A Guide to Amos
5. Church History 1: The First Advance AD 29–500
6. A Guide to Psalms
7. Old Testament Introduction 1: History of Israel
8. Church History 2: Setback and Recovery AD 500–1500
9. Applied Theology 1: 'Go . . . and make disciples'
10. Old Testament Introduction 2: The Books of the Old Testament
11. A Guide to Romans
12. A Guide to Religions
13. A Guide to Exodus
14. Church History 3: New Movements AD 1500–1800
15. Old Testament Theology 3: Theology of the Old Testament
16. A Guide to Isaiah 40–66
17. A Guide to 1 Corinthians
18. A Guide to Philippians
19. Applied Theology 2: 'Tend my sheep'
20. A Guide to the Revelation
21. A Guide to Isaiah 1–39
22. Church History 4: Christian Worldwide AD 1800 Onwards
23. A Reader in African Christian Theology (A)
24. New Testament Introduction 1: Jesus Christ: His Life and His Church
25. A New Teaching, A New Learning: A Guide to Teaching Theology (A)
26. New Testament Introduction 2: The Formation of the Christian Scriptures
27. A Guide to Acts
28. A Guide to Galatians

IN PREPARATION

A Guide to Deuteronomy
A Guide to Jeremiah
A Guide to Hosea
The Inter-Testamental Period
Readings in Indian Christian Theology (A)

TEF Study Guide 18

A GUIDE TO PHILIPPIANS

John Hargreaves

First published in 1983
SPCK
Holy Trinity Church
Marylebone Road
London NW1 4DU

Reprinted with amendments 1991

ACKNOWLEDGEMENTS

Unless otherwise stated, the Scripture quotations in this publication are from the Revised Standard Version of the Bible, Ecumenical Edition, copyrighted 1973 by the Division of Christian Education of the National Council of the Churches of Christ in the USA.

The pictures are reproduced by courtesy of the Mansell Collection (p. 27), Mr Carlos Reyes (p. 35), the Federal Theological Seminary of Southern Africa (p. 65), and Camera Press Ltd.

ISBN 0 281 04019 2 (net edition)
ISBN 0 281 04020 6 (non-net edition for Africa, Asia,
S. Pacific and Caribbean)

Printed in Great Britain by
Dotesios Ltd, Trowbridge, Wilts

Contents

Preface

Some years ago in Ibadan, five Nigerian students stayed in College during vacation and studied Philippians. The interpretations they gave and the questions they asked stimulated me to attempt to write up our discussion in the form of a commentary. This was done, but other work held up its completion. Now, thirty years later, I have rewritten and completed it, without, I hope, losing sight of the original contributions. My thanks, therefore, are due first of all to these five 'students', who are (if I remember rightly): Canon R. I. Aiyejoto, Archdeacon D. O. Aroso, Canon Dr W. O. Ajayi, Archdeacon Z. O. Banwo, and Archdeadon M. D. Oyinlade.

I should also like to thank:

My brother Cecil Hargreaves, who shared with me some of his insights into the meaning of Philippians arising from his experience of India and from his contacts with Dr C. F. D. Moule;

My son Jonathan for the paragraph about richer and poorer nations on p. 133 of the revised edition;

Mr Stephen Ridout, who most helpfully filled many pages with suggested corrections and amendments;

Rabbi John D. Rayner, who was kind enough to give me information concerning the Jewish religion;

The Community of St Julian's, Coolham, England who provided wonderful surroundings for work; Daphne Terry, who as editor has now given me kindly incentive and encouragement for over twenty years; and Elizabeth Spence for most carefully and expeditiously typing the original manuscript.

JOHN HARGREAVES

Using this Guide

In the Introductory Note (p. 1) we consider the reasons why Paul wrote to the Philippian Christians as he did, and why it is important for us to study his letter today. But before beginning their study, readers may find it helpful to consider how they can make the best use of this book to guide them.

Each section of the Guide consists of:

1. An *Introduction* in which the Bible passage is briefly summarized so as to make quite clear what chief subjects Paul was dealing with, and the most important message he was sending to the Philippians about them. Of course, reading this Introduction is not meant to take the place of reading the actual passage in the Bible. We need to read carefully the words of the Bible itself at each stage of our study.

2. *Notes* on particular words or verses which seem to need explanation or discussion, with detailed *Interpretation* of the passage, in which we discuss what it meant to the Philippians of Paul's time, and how we should understand and apply it to our own lives as Christians today.

3. *Suggestions* for revision and further study.

SPECIAL WORD STUDIES

The notes include special studies of the many important Bible words which Paul used in this letter. The list on p. 138 shows where these words are chiefly discussed and the Index references to the studies are given in bold type.

STUDY SUGGESTIONS

These suggestions for further study appear at the end of each section. They are intended to help readers who are working alone to study more thoroughly and understand Paul's teaching more clearly, and to check their own progress. They can also be used in the classroom or at seminars, and provide topics for group research and discussion. They are of four kinds:

1. *Words:* These are to help readers check and deepen their understanding of some important words and phrases, especially those discussed in the Special Word Studies.

2. *Content:* These are intended to help readers check the work they have done and make sure they have fully grasped the ideas and points of teaching given.
3. *Bible:* These relate the ideas and teaching in Paul's letter with ideas and teaching found in other parts of the Bible.
4. *Discussion and research:* These are intended to help readers think out the practical applications of Paul's teaching to their own lives and to the mission of the Church in the world. They are especially suitable for use by a group.

The best way to use these study suggestions is: first, re-read the Bible passage itself; secondly, read the appropriate section of the Guide carefully once or twice; and lastly, do the work suggested, in writing or group discussion, without looking at the Guide again except where there is an instruction to do so.

The *Key* at the end of the book (p. 139) will enable readers to check their work on those questions which can be checked in this way. In most cases the Key does not give the answer to a question: it shows where an answer is to be found, either in the Guide or in the Bible.

All these study suggestions are only *suggestions*. But in some cases they provide further interpretation of Paul's letter. Some teachers will want to select only those which are relevant to a particular situation, or may prefer to substitute questions of their own.

INDEX

The Index (p. 147) includes only proper names and the more important words and ideas which occur in the Letter to the Philippians or which are discussed in the Guide.

BIBLE VERSION

The English translation of the Bible used in the Guide is the *Revised Standard Version of the Bible: Ecumenical Edition* (RSV). The *New English Bible* (NEB) and *Good News Bible* (GNB) are used in a few cases where they show the meaning more clearly. Other translations mentioned are the Authorized (or 'King James') *Version* (AV), the *Jerusalem Bible* (JB), and those by James Moffatt and J. B. Phillips.

FURTHER READING

The Bibliography on p. ix lists some books which readers may find useful for further study of Philippians.

Bibliography

William Barclay, *Philippians, Colossians and Thessalonians*. St Andrew's Press.

F. W. Beare, *Philippians*. A. & C. Black Ltd.

Kenneth Grayston, *Philippians, Thessalonians* (Cambridge NEB Commentaries). Cambridge University Press.

J. L. Houlden, *Paul's Letters from Prison*. SCM/Pelican.

R. P. Martin, *Philippians* (Tyndale New Testament Commentaries). Inter-Varsity Press.

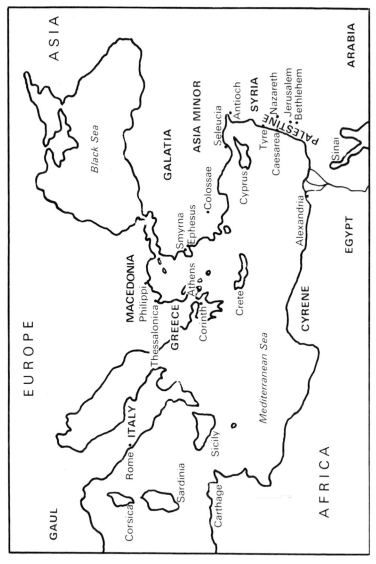

The Eastern Mediterranean in Paul's time.

Introductory Note
Why Write? Why Read?

WHY DID PAUL WRITE THIS LETTER?

Paul wrote to the Philippians chiefly in order to maintain and strengthen the friendship which began when he first visited Philippi. Philippi was an important city in Macedonia, in the north of Greece, and Paul visited it in about AD 52. We read in Acts 16.11–40 how he first preached to a small group beside the river, and then built up the Christian congregation there until he had to leave because of violent demonstrations against his teaching. He paid two more visits, probably in AD 57 and 58 (Acts 20.1 and 20.6). During this time the congregation had been growing. They knew that they owed their existence as a congregation to Paul, and they kept in touch with him by letters. When he needed help for poor Jews in Judea, they sent him money. When he himself was in prison, they sent him a gift. There was real friendship between Paul and the Christians at Philippi, as we see from verses such as 1.7; 2.12; 4.1.

No one knows in which city Paul was in prison when he wrote this letter. Some think that it was in Ephesus or Caesarea, but more probably he wrote from Rome (see note on 1.13). He had gone to Jerusalem to take the present from Gentile Christians to Jewish Christians, but again there were clashes on account of his teaching, and he was arrested (Acts 21.17–39). He hoped to get a fair trial by appealing to Caesar, and so he was sent to Rome and was in prison there from AD 60–62. So far as we know he was never brought to trial. According to a tradition he died in AD 64.

Paul had other special reasons for writing. For example, he wanted to encourage the Philippians, who knew that he was still in prison and were beginning to lose heart. They realized that he might be condemned to death. So he wrote to tell them that, although he was suffering the pain of imprisonment, and indeed might soon be killed, the prison was an excellent place from which to preach the gospel (1.12–14), and so he was full of joy (1.18).

Paul needed also to tell the Philippians about one of their own members, Epaphroditus. They had sent Epaphroditus with a gift for Paul, and to comfort him, but while he was with Paul Epaphroditus fell ill and nearly died. News of his illness had reached Philippi and the congregation were becoming anxious. So, as soon as Epaphroditus had

1

recovered, Paul sent him back to Philippi with his thanks and with this letter (2.25–30).

A third special reason for Paul's writing was the urgent need for unity in the congregation. He wrote in order to bring divided people together again (2.1–4). He had heard of members being divided for various reasons: (a) There seem to have been Jews in Philippi who were persuading one section of the congregation to forget the 'new way' which Paul had preached and to keep the traditional Jewish regulations (3.2–11). (b) Others were claiming to have developed further in the Christian life than they really had, and were thinking of themselves as 'superior' (3.12–16). And (c) there was division because two leading members of the congregation, both of them women, could not work happily together (4.2, 3).

WHY DO WE READ THIS LETTER?

We read it because it is an opportunity of opening ourselves to the same living Spirit who moved Paul to write it and who led him to live as he lived. We read it because we are in need of that living Spirit.

This is, of course, true of the other New Testament books. But there are special reasons for choosing to read this letter to the Philippians.

First, because we live at a time when very many Christians are suffering for their faith, as Paul suffered. Not only have Church leaders such as Archbishop Romero of El Salvador and Archbishop Luwum of Uganda been martyred during the time when this Guide was being written, but countless numbers of unnamed Christians of every continent have suffered because of their commitment to Jesus Christ. We need to remember that the letter we are studying was written by a Christian who was in prison because of his beliefs to Christians who were also suffering for their beliefs. If we who read this letter have suffered or are suffering for the same reason, we are in a special position to understand the most important parts of it. We may also be helped to see our own sufferings as pain which we can share with Christ Himself (3.10).

Secondly, we read this letter because of the urgent need today of unity among Christians, in order that the Church may effectively preach peace and reconciliation to a divided world. Why should the world which needs to be united take seriously a Church which is itself disunited? So this letter is of special importance. Paul wrote it out of his own close fellowship with the Philippians, and, as we have seen, in order to point the way to unity among Christians.

Thirdly, we read it because we, like Paul, are uncertain about our future, the future of our country and the future of mankind. Unlike Paul, we are often anxious and afraid. So we are strengthened by reading of Paul's confidence that, whatever may happen, God has the future under His control. See the note on 1.6 about 'the day of the Lord'.

Another reason why many people read this letter is because it is a very good introduction to Paul's other letters. It contains in a short space many of the important ideas which we find in his other letters, and forty or fifty of the most important words.

But Paul did not write this letter in order to educate his readers in the meaning of words. Nor is this our chief reason for reading it. As we have seen, we read it above all in order to place ourselves alongside those who first read it, and to expose ourselves to the love and the authority of the same Lord. This is the chief purpose of all Bible study.

1.1,2

Greetings and a Prayer

INTRODUCTION

In the days when Paul wrote, this was the usual way in which to begin a letter, by giving the names of the writer and the addressee, and then a greeting. If we are using the RSV, verse 1 may not look like a letter. In a modern translation we might express it as follows: 'Dear Christians of Philippi, greetings from Timothy and myself, slaves of Christ Jesus. Greetings to you all, you who are God's dedicated people in fellowship with Christ Jesus. Greetings to your overseers and their assistants.'

Then after this greeting, Paul added a prayer in v. 2: 'May God our Father and the Lord Jesus Christ give you grace and peace.'

In these verses we notice especially:

1. Paul was showing his friendship with the Philippians rather than his authority over them. In most of his letters he reminded his readers of the authority which God had given him to speak and work in His name. He often described himself as an 'Apostle': 'Paul, a servant of Jesus Christ, called to be an apostle . . . to all God's beloved in Rome' (Rom. 1.1–7). He used the Greek word '*apostolos*' in this letter, too, in 2.25 (where the RSV translates it as 'messenger'). But before he wrote anything else he made it clear to his readers that he was writing as a friend.

2. Paul used the name of Jesus Christ three times in these two verses. From the start of this letter he was reminding the Philippians that living 'in Christ' was the great experience which he and they shared. Paul was a Jew, and since childhood had believed in God. But God had come into the world in Jesus Christ, and since that event the fullest life was a life lived in Christ (see note on 4.10).

Note: Paul mentioned Timothy in v. 1 because Timothy was with him at the time, and because Timothy was well known to the Christians of Philippi (see notes on 2.19–22). Timothy did not take any share in writing the letter.

NOTES AND INTERPRETATION

Servants of Christ Jesus (v. 1a): The Greek word '*doulos*' is translated 'servant' here, but it is the ordinary word for 'slave'. In the days when Paul wrote, it was the custom for all households to have one or more slaves. But why did Paul call himself and Timothy 'Christ's slaves'? In what way is a Christian Christ's 'slave'?

1. A Christian is a slave *to Christ*, but not to other men and women. Nor is he a slave to traditions or to his own habits. This is what Paul meant in Romans 6.22: 'Now that you have been set free from sin and have become slaves of God, the return you get is . . . eternal life.'

2. He is *owned* by Christ. The owner bought his slaves and then possessed them just as he possessed his home. In 1 Corinthians 6.19, 20 Paul says, 'You are not your own: you have been bought' (by Christ).

3. Therefore he is *obedient* to this one master, Christ, and to no-one else. But a Christian is unlike a slave of those days because he is free to obey or disobey.

4. A slave's master gave him *protection* and safety. When the great Bishop Polycarp was arrested by Roman soldiers in AD 156, he was told that he could be set free if he would speak against Christ. He said, 'I have bccn the slave of Christ for 86 years and He has never treated me unfairly. How can I blaspheme against my King who has kept me safe?'

In this verse Paul wrote about himself and Timothy being slaves to Christ and serving Him. Later in the letter he had much to say about Christians serving one another (2.1–4) and about Christ Himself being a servant (2.5–11).

To all the saints in Christ Jesus (v. 1b): The word 'saint' usuallv has a different meaning today from the meaning it had for Paul. It does not here mean 'very good people'. For this reason it may be better to translate it 'God's dedicated people'. The Greek word is '*hagios*' which is often translated 'holy'.

1. For Paul 'saints' were:

(a) Those who had been *set apart* or consecrated by God for a special purpose. Saints who are 'in Christ Jesus' have been dedicated to do what He wants doing. The word 'holy' was used like this in the Old Testament: 'You are a people holy to the Lord your God. The Lord has chosen you . . .' (Deut. 7.6). The Israelites were 'holy' and 'chosen' in spite of their many failures and sins. This is why Paul could call the Philippians 'saints'. They were ordinary people, but God had given them special work to do.

(b) Those who had *accepted* the privilege of being chosen in this way. We are not born 'saints'. We are not 'saints' merely for the reason that our parents were.

2. Later on the word 'saint' also came to be used in a different way. It began to mean extra-ordinary people, those whom others regarded as living unusually Christ-like lives. So on All Saints Day Christians praise God for such people of the past.

3. It is of course important that we should take note of these great Christians and thank God for them. But it is dangerous to use the same word for them as we use for the people whom Paul called 'saints' in this verse.

The danger is that we, the ordinary but committed Christians of today, will be disheartened because we are admiring the lives of extraordinary Christians and feeling we can never be like them. If this happens, there is a further danger: that we shall forget what God expects from us and what we are capable of becoming.

4. Christians need to accept the title of 'saint' so that they may remember that God has set them apart for a purpose and given them a commission. Therefore they accept the suffering that follows (as Paul and the Philippians did). On a Sunday they are with their fellow-Christians in church, while their friends who do not belong to the Church are perhaps fishing, or sleeping, or playing football. Christians often have the pain of losing friends for this reason. They know that they are different in this way. But they also know that this 'being different' does not mean that they are superior to other people. 'Saints' have to be in the world and yet not of it. It is not always easy to find a balance between the two.

Note: The words 'saints-in-Christ-Jesus' should be taken together. The meaning is, 'Those who are in fellowship with Christ Jesus and have been set apart by God for a special purpose.' See note on 4.10 for the phrase 'in-Christ'.

Who are at Philippi (v. 1c):

(a) The 'saints' or 'Christians' to whom Paul was writing were probably meeting in someone's house. (Perhaps they needed two houses to meet in, because the numbers had grown too big for one house.) We can picture the scene as it may have been:

It is Sunday and they have gathered from different parts of the city to celebrate the presence of the risen Jesus Christ. It is a mixed congregation, containing both Jews and Gentiles. As there is not much room, some are sitting on a bed, and most are standing. The service begins with prayers and readings, and then the leader breaks the bread and pours the wine, and the members share the life of God, and are strengthened to go out to serve Him in the world. But before they do so, someone says, 'Paul has sent us a letter and I will read it to you!'

(b) What sort of city was it in which they met? It was an old city, originally built by the Thracians who lived in the north of Greece. It became famous when Philip, King of Macedonia and the father of Alexander the Great, refounded it and gave it his name. It was important to him because of its gold-mines, and because the great main road from the East to Western Europe passed through it. Later it was part of the Roman Empire. The Romans erected great buildings in it, which Paul saw, and some of which visitors can see today, e.g. the open air theatre on the mountainside.

When Paul saw Philippi the population was very mixed. There were Thracians (the original inhabitants), Greeks, Romans (many of whom were retired soldiers), and people from many different parts of the Roman Empire. There was also a handful of Jews. Consequently there were many different religions and 'gods' in Philippi: the Thracian 'god' 'Father Freedom' and the 'goddess' Bendix; the Greek 'Athena'; the Roman Jupiter, Mars, and the Emperor; and the Egyptian 'gods', Isis, Serapis, and Harpocrates.

It was in this sort of a city, among so many different races and religions, that the tiny group of Christians met.

With the bishops and deacons (v. 1d): At the time when Paul was writing, the Greek word '*episcopos*' (translated 'bishop' here), was used for any 'overseer'. The Greek word '*diakonos*' ('deacon') was used for any helper or servant. So Paul was sending his greetings to those members of the congregation who looked after the arrangements for Church services and the money that was given.

Later on the Church grew in numbers and was more fully organized. Then the words were used in a different way. '*Episcopos*' described the person who had authority to preside at Holy Communion, was responsible for the congregation, and protected it in time of persecution. '*Diakonos*' was then used to describe the person who assisted him in this work.

Bishop: Later still, one '*episcopos*' was chosen to be responsible for a group of congregations, and became more and more a *governor* (i.e. the sort of position held by 'bishops' in many Churches today).

Most Christians today agree that some people must be given the authority to lead the Church. But they do not all agree as to what sort of authority God wants His Church leaders to have, or what sort of work they should do. (This is one important reason why Churches find it difficult to unite.)

Some say that the only sort of *episcopos* that God intends is the leader of a single congregation. Others say that it is God's will that an *episcopos* should be responsible for a group of congregations.

In some Churches he is able to be a pastoral overseer, who knows all those over whom he has authority; in other Churches he is given so much work of administration to do that it is difficult for him to do a pastor's work as well.

In all Churches he has important decisions to take, especially decisions concerning the declaring of the true Christian teaching in the face of false teaching. But in some Churches he takes most of these decisions on his own, while in others he acts in consultation with other leaders.

Some Churches expect their 'bishops' or leaders to be involved in political affairs on behalf of the Church; other Churches do not want them to do this.

We do not settle this problem (concerning the sort of authority which God wants Church leaders to have) simply by referring to this verse or any other New Testament verses. We can only settle it when Christians meet together and allow the living Spirit of God to guide them.

Deacon: The Greek word itself means 'one who serves'. Paul used it to refer to Christ Himself (Rom. 15.8), to himself (1 Cor. 3.5), and to his assistants in the work of evangelism such as Timothy (1 Thess. 3.2).

The work of a deacon changed as the needs of the Church changed, and today different Churches use the word 'deacon' to mean different things. But its meaning of 'the one who serves' has remained, following the example of Christ: 'the Son of man came not to be served but to serve' (Mark 10.45). See note on 2.7.

Grace and peace (v. 2): This verse, as we have seen, is a prayer: 'May you experience God's *grace*', i.e. 'may you discover for yourselves that God treats you better than you deserve' (see note on 1.29). 'May you be given that *peace* by which God brings you into fellowship with Himself and with other people.'

Although this is a prayer, it is also a greeting, or rather a mixture of two greetings. The ordinary Greek greeting was '*Charis!*' ('Grace!'), and the ordinary Jewish greeting was, and still is, '*Shalom!*' ('Peace!').

Thus Paul used two words which were commonly used by those who were not Christians, so that it became customary for Christians to use them in a new way. In the same way, Church leaders in non-Christian countries today often try to make use of old, non-Christian words and customs, rather than invent new ones. Someone who is translating the Bible into the language of a newly-converted tribe or people often tries to use the word for God which that tribe already uses, unless of course it will lead to entirely wrong ideas about God. When they are finding music to use in worship, they often try to use music which the people know, unless it is connected with evil practices.

God our Father and the Lord Jesus Christ (v. 2):

1. 'God our Father': the God whom Jesus Christ taught us to call 'Our Father' (Matt. 6.9). The Jews said that God was like a 'father' because among them (as among most peoples today) the father, not the mother, is the head of the family. But this name does not mean that God is male rather than female. In some countries today (but not in all) it would be just as useful to call God 'Mother'.

2. By writing the word 'and' before the name of Jesus, Paul did not mean that Jesus was separate or different from God. He was saying 'As I pray that God will give you His grace and peace, I remind you that this God made Himself known to us by becoming man, the man Jesus.'

STUDY SUGGESTIONS

WORDS

1. The Greek word is translated 'servant' here, but it is the ordinary word for 'slave'.
   (a) Which do you think is better? Give reasons for your answer.
   (b) What word is used in this verse in another language which you know? What meaning does that word have for an ordinary reader?
2. 'Paul used words which were commonly used by those who were not Christians, so that it became customary for Christians to use them in a new way' (p. 8). What word does your Church usually use for 'God'? Is it (a) a word also used by non-Christians, or (b) was it imported from outside? What are the advantages and disadvantages of (a) and (b)?

CONTENT

3. When did Paul first become friends with the Philippians?
4. (a) What were the advantages of being a slave at the time when Paul wrote?
   (b) Why did he write in Gal. 4.7 that Christians were no longer like slaves?
5. What are the two most important truths about a 'saint'?
6. What did the words 'bishop' and 'deacon' mean at the time when Paul was writing?

BIBLE

7. What is the chief difference between the beginning of this letter (vv 1 and 2) and the beginning of the letter to the Galatians (vv 1–3)?
8. In the following passages the word 'saint' (or 'holy' or 'sacred') occurs in most translations. To what or whom did the writer refer in each case?
   (a) Exod. 3.5 (b) Exod. 20.8. (c) Psalm 132.16. (d) Acts 26.10. (e) Phil. 1.1. (f) 2 Tim. 3.15.
9. 'God our Father' (v. 2). Read Isaiah 49.14, 15; 66.12, 13; Hosea 11.1–3. Do you think that, in the light of such verses, God should be called 'mother' as well as 'father'? Give reasons for your answer.

9

DISCUSSION AND RESEARCH

10. ' "Saints" have to be (1) in the world, and (2) yet not of it. It is not always easy to find a balance between the two' (p. 6).
    (a) Which of the two do you think Christians tend to be in your Church?
    (b) In your Church do you revere any local 'saints' of the past, *or* none at all, *or* those traditionally revered by all Christians?
11. 'Bishops' (1.1).
    (a) What title or titles do you give your Church leaders?
    (b) How important are these titles?
    (c) How do the leaders take their decisions? Is it mainly as individuals or in company with others?
    (d) How far are they able to combine administration with pastoral work?
12. 'Grace and peace' (1.2). What are the most common words used in greetings in your own language? Is 'peace' or 'grace' one of them?
13. 'Paul was writing as a friend' (p. 4).
    (a) What made Paul and the Philippians friends?
    (b) What drew together you and your closest friends?

1.3–8

Thanksgiving for Partnership

INTRODUCTION

Here Paul was telling his friends at Philippi something about himself and his thoughts about them. He said four things:

1. I am praying for you (vv 3, 4);
2. I am thanking God for you, especially for your generosity (vv 3,5);
3. I am like you, because we have both been generously treated by God (v. 7);
4. I am longing to see you (v. 8).

We notice first the *joy* which Paul showed in writing this. When we remember that he was writing from prison it seems wonderful that he could write with such thankfulness and joy. We may feel that if we ourselves had been in Paul's place we might have been more likely to express our anxiety concerning the future, or concerning the health of Epaphroditus.

What made Paul able to write in the way that he did? Many verses in this letter provide the answer, e.g. vv 5 and 6.

We notice again that Paul who was their leader in the Church wrote as a friend to other friends: 'I hold you in my heart' (v. 7). Somehow he was able to join the *authority* (which he believed God had given him) with this *friendliness*. Those who received his letter would, as a result, be happy to consider seriously what he wrote. Their attitude to him would be very different from our attitude as we read a notice on a school notice-board, or look at advertisements placed on the roadside by someone who wishes us to buy his cigarettes; it would be different from the attitude of people who stand listening to a military governor making announcements on the radio.

NOTES AND INTERPRETATION

My God (v. 3): These may seem to be the words of a greedy or selfish person, as if he was saying, 'God is mine, not yours'. But what Paul meant was that in the loneliness of the prison he had a companion, God Himself. God was his, not someone whom his ancestors had worshipped long ago. God was someone who was around him and to whom he himself had become a willing slave, and with whom he had a special relationship. Each child in a family has a different relationship with his father, no matter how many brothers and sisters he has. So he says 'my father', rather than 'our father'.

The writers of the Psalms used the same language: 'The Lord is *my* Shepherd' (Ps. 23); 'O God, thou art *my* God; early will I seek thee' (Ps. 63, AV).

It is true that Jesus taught us to say 'Our Father', not 'My Father'. It is true that whenever we pray to God and serve Him, we do so as members of His Church. Yet there are things that I (and no one else in the world) can say to God, just because I am myself; there is no one who has my joys and my temptations. And there are things that God is wanting me (and no one else) to do. So I too can say, 'My God'.

You all (vv 4, 7, 8) – 'every prayer of mine for you all': It is clear that 'you all' are important words because Paul uses them four times in these few verses. He was writing to *all* the members of this small congregation, the uneducated as well as the well-educated, those who had opposed him and those who had agreed with him, those whom it was difficult to like and those whom it was easy to like. He wrote 'you all' in order to help them to see themselves as one body, and to prevent division among them.

We also see from these words how wide was Paul's concern for other people. He included 'all' when he was preaching, Gentiles as well as Jews; he did not exclude anyone. 'I try to please all in ... everything I do ... that they may be saved' (1 Cor. 10.33).

A Christian today prays for other people of whose needs he has learnt: not because he agrees with them or likes them, but because all are equally in need of God and in need of each other. See note on 'Prayer' in 4.6b.

Your partnership (v. 5): Paul was writing this letter partly because the Philippian Christians needed deeper 'partnership' amongst themselves. So it is not surprising that he used the Greek word translated 'partnership' six times. But this 'partnership' (or 'fellowship') was also something which he valued very highly for himself. He was in prison and was separated from other Christians, and the Philippians supported him and were his 'partners'.

The Greek word is '*koinonia*'. As there is no one English word which can be used to translate it (except perhaps the new word 'togetherness'), it is best to use the Greek word itself. What does it mean to say that a group of Christians can have '*koinonia*'?

1. It means that each of them has *koinonia with God*, through Christ. This is the thought in 2.1 and in 3.10.

2. As a result, they have *koinonia with each other*. This is what Paul was saying in this verse, and in 1.7; 2.1; 4.14; and 4.15.

It is important to understand that the *koinonia* which Christians enjoy with each other is a result of having roots. The 'roots' are the *koinonia* which each has with God. We can see why one must follow from the other. When each Christian knows that he is accepted by the loving God just as he is, then he is able to accept other Christians just as they are. So there is *koinonia* amongst them. They can trust each other. They can allow each other to hold different opinions. They can speak freely with each other. They can forgive each other. But someone who does not believe that he is accepted into fellowship with God is unable to accept others in this way.

Note that sometimes the 'roots' and the 'result' are thought of together 'The fellowship of the Holy Spirit' (2 Cor. 13.14) means 'fellowship with God Holy Spirit' *and also* 'the fellowship with other Christians which God Holy Spirit has created'. So in the Holy Communion Service (the Holy *Koinonia*) each Christian has communion with God *and also* communion with his fellow worshippers.

3. When Christians share work, they have a special opportunity to experience *koinonia*, like two partners who own a shop and work in it. They have *koinonia* if they have the same sins. In 1.5 Paul reminded the Philippians that he and they had been sharing work for ten years, ever since they met in Philippi (Acts 16.12). In 1.7 he said, 'When I appear in the dock to vouch for the truth of the gospel, you all share in the privilege that is mine' (NEB).

In one town Methodists, Roman Catholics, and Anglicans (who knew that they all had fellowship with God through Jesus Christ) joined in the work of visiting every house in the town. In this way, their *koinonia* was increased.

In the same way, *koinonia* is strong when the members of a group share suffering or danger. The players in a Salvation Army band in Nairobi were once playing hymns and preaching in a district where there were no Christians at that time. The crowd was treating their visit as a sort of game, in which the object was to make the band go away as soon as possible by throwing tins and shouting and singing. At the end of the evening a member of the band said, 'We may not have been given any converts. Who knows? But we have certainly been given fellowship amongst ourselves!'

4. Their *koinonia* is shown when each *shares in a practical* way what each possesses (see 4.15). In Romans 15.26 the 'contribution for the poor' which some Christians sent was actually called '*the koinonia*'.

So today Christians of one country show their *koinonia* with those of another country by each contributing to the needs of the others. A West African priest came to work for a time in an English town, and after he had left a member of the congregation said, 'We have been giving to the Church in Africa for many years. Now we are receiving. This African has lived among us a life of such joy that he has given us something we shall never forget.'

5. *Koinonia* exists even *when members are separated.* *Koinonia* among Christians does not die when some of the Christians die: we may call this the 'Communion of the Saints'. It was the same truth that made a Japanese student in America able to be at peace during the whole of his three-year course although he was separated from his wife and family. He said, 'We are all united in Christ.'

6. It is *koinonia* among Christians which (more than anything else) draws non-Christians into the Church, and into a belief in God's love. There is an Indian lecturer in a Christian College in Birmingham who was a Muslim when he came to England some years ago. Through his work he met a group of Christian students, and he says that it was because of the fellowship, love, and honesty that existed between them that he began to take the gospel seriously, and later became a Christian himself.

7. The deepest *koinonia* often comes when the group which is working together (whether building or studying the Bible) is a small one. Perhaps this is one reason why Jesus chose only twelve disciples.

The gospel (vv 5 and 7): Seven times in this letter Paul wrote about the 'good news' or the 'gospel'. (These are translations of the Greek word '*evangelion*').

The word is used in different ways:

(a) The message *which Jesus preached*, when He said that God was now in control of mankind in a new way. 'Jesus came proclaiming the

13

'Thankful for your partnership in the gospel' (1.5). 'When Christians share work, they have a special opportunity to experience partnership (or *koinonia*)' (p. 12).

The partnership of this man and this woman, picking tea in India, is a parable of partnership between Christians. What examples of this can you give from your experience as a Church member? What, in your experience, prevents it from happening?

Gospel of God . . . "The kingdom of God is upon you"' (Mark 1.14, 15, NEB). 'The gospel of the grace of God' (Acts 20.24).

(b) The preaching *about* Jesus, in which His followers declared that He died and rose again. Paul's work was to defend this 'good news' and declare its truth ('defence and confirmation' v. 7).

(c) *A book* in which was written the story of Jesus. So we speak of 'St Mark's Gospel'.

(d) The whole *work* of preaching and travelling and caring for congregations which Paul did in obedience to God. This is how Paul usually used the word in this letter, e.g. 4.15: 'In the beginning of the gospel, when I left Macedonia.'

It is useful to translate it 'good news' because each of these two words tells us something important:

1. It is a *good* message to preach and *good* work to be doing. So cheer up!

2. It is *news*. At every moment of every day someone somewhere is hearing it for the first time. Every generation needs to be told it afresh. And Christians can go on discovering more of the truth in it as long as they live.

He who began a good work in you will bring it to completion (v. 6a): God, in His love, made Himself known to the men and women of Philippi, and they loved Him in return and so the Church there was begun. This is the 'beginning' which God did (using Paul to do it). But God had not left the Philippians alone: He would continue to work in and around them, so that they might increase in their love to Him and to each other. (Some people think that Paul was saying, 'God has helped you to send me some money: now He will help you to finish the good work and send me a lot more money.' But this is not the meaning!)

So Paul wrote this verse:

(a) In order to give encouragement to the Philippians; and we see from 1.28, 29 how much they needed it. He was showing them that God would not neglect them. (This is encouragement which thousands of lonely little congregations need today.) (b) In order to remind them that Christians should be developing and growing in their devotion to God.

1. These are words for any group of Christians working in Christ's Name today. The chaplain of a Christian hospital in Pakistan has written: 'Often in a hospital like ours we are just the first link in leading someone to Christ. We will never know when or where the next link may be forged. We are certain that God will provide the link. Or sometimes someone comes who has heard the Gospel elsewhere and we have the privilege of being used as a further link. At other times we are allowed the joy of being the last link before a person's

baptism. ... So we are not worried, or burdened, or insisting on knowing how our work will work out.'

2. They are also words for individual Christians. First, they show that we cannot complete our own lives as Christians. Someone who had a very good watch said, 'From time to time it needs mending. But it can't do it for itself, and I can't do it. I have to take it to the maker.' So Christians take themselves to their Maker.

Secondly, a Christian knows that he must be as patient with himself as God is. It will not help if he gets angry with himself. The completing will take a long time. Changes will be needed and will not be easy to accept. It is like the story of a crab's life. A crab has to grow a great many different shells over its body before it is fully grown. As the crab's body grows, so that the hard shell is too small to hold the body, the crab throws the shell off and grows a larger one. But until the new shell has grown the soft crab is in danger of being attacked by enemies. Its growing process is a long one.

It is not the job of Christians to complete God's work in the world. Their work is to prepare themselves and others; but the completion, the end, is in God's hands, as we see in the second part of this same verse.

At the day of Jesus Christ (v. 6b): Paul often spoke and wrote about this 'day' and called it by different names: 'the day of the Lord' (1 Cor. 5.5); 'that day' (2 Thess. 1.10); 'the Day' (1 Cor. 3.13); etc.

What is this 'day of the Lord'? It is the time when God will complete the work which He began with the creation.

1. Those who expect this day are therefore strengthened in their difficulties and pains. They are like people making a long journey on foot. These travellers are tired as they follow a road through a long hot valley. But they know that there will come a time in the evening when they reach the village on the mountainside: then they will look down the road where they had been so hot and tired.

We already know that God is in control. (Jesus taught us this when He spoke of God as a 'King'.) We also know, if we understand this word 'day', that nothing can ever prevent God from finishing what He has planned to do.

2. Those who expect this 'day' are also aware that this world is not permanent. They are like a man who lived in a part of Ethiopia where earthquakes often happen. He said he was always aware that life was not permanent and that he had to take seriously the words of Jesus: 'Do not be anxious about tomorrow' (Matt. 6.34). He had to discover how to live now, not how he could live next year. See Hebrews 3.13: 'Exhort one another every day, as long as it is called "today".'
Note that:

(a) There are two special ways in which God's 'finishing' is described in the New Testament: as the 'coming' of Jesus Christ (although we cannot know how He will come), and as God's 'judgement' of all mankind.

(b) From this it is clear that the 'day' is not the same as the time when all human beings will cease to live on the earth. Such a time will come. It may come because men totally destroy each other by bombs. It may come because the sun's heat becomes too great. But this is not the same as the 'day'.

(c) Again, the 'day' does not mean the time of a Christian's own death.

When will this 'day' come? At one time Paul thought that it would come very soon indeed. See 1 Thessalonians 4.15: 'We who are left alive until the Lord comes . . .' (NEB). Later he wrote as if it would not come for a long time. The truth is that we do not know the time. See Mark 13.32: 'of that day . . . no one knows, not even the angels in heaven, nor the Son, but only the Father.' What is important is that we should live every day in readiness for it. If we live like this we have confidence (in God): we act with responsibility (towards God).

Paul wrote of 'the day' partly because there were some Christians who were claiming that they had already been made perfect, and that there was nothing left that God had to do.

You are all partakers with me of grace (v. 7): The Philippians and Paul were both privileged to receive God's grace. Both they and he knew that although they were suffering, God was giving them gifts which were more than they deserved. This is always the main thought in the word 'grace'. See note on 1.29.

The translation 'you are all partakers of my grace' (AV) has misled many readers.

STUDY SUGGESTIONS

WORDS
1. (a) The Greek word '*koinonia*' is translated 'partnership' in v. 5 (see p. 12). Which 5 of the following words have the same or nearly the same meaning as 'partnership'?
      sharing   partiality   communion   acceptance
      service   fellowship   participation   compulsion
   (b) What is the difference between *koinonia* and friendliness?
   (c) How is *koinonia* translated in another language which you know? What is its literal meaning?
2. (a) What word do we find in 1.3 and also in Pss. 23.1 and 63.1?
   (b) Why is it singular and not plural in 1.3?

CONTENT

3. What made Paul able to write with joy although he was in prison?
4. (a) How many times in vv 3–8 did Paul use the phrase 'you all'?
   (b) Why did he repeat it?
5. What do the following verses tell us about Paul's relationship with the Philippian Christians?
   v. 3; vv 5, 6; v. 7.
6. What did Paul mean by the 'completion' of God's work (v. 6a)? What did he *not* mean?

BIBLE

7. Say whether *koinonia* ('fellowship', 'partnership') refers to (i) fellowship with God or (ii) fellowship with one another or (iii) a sign of fellowship, in each of the following verses:
   (a) Acts 2.42 (b) Rom. 15:26 (c) 1 Cor. 10.16
   (d) 2 Cor. 9.13 (e) Gal. 2.9 (f) 1 John 1.6
8. What did the writer of each of the following passages say about the 'gospel' (1.5, 1.7)?
   (a) Mark 13.10 (b) Rom. 1.16 (c) Rom. 10.16
   (d) 1 Cor. 9.16 (e) 1 Cor 15.1, 2
9. What did Paul mean by 'the day of Jesus Christ' (v. 6)?
10. What is the day of Jesus Christ called in each of the following verses?
    (a) Rom. 2.16 (b) 1 Cor. 1.8 (c) Eph. 4.30
    (d) 1 Thess. 5.2 (e) 1 Thess 5.4 (f) 2 Thess. 2.2

DISCUSSION AND RESEARCH

11. 'Partnership' (v. 5).
    (a) With whom do Christians have *koinonia*?
    (b) What event or events have most helped members of your congregation to experience 'partnership' together during the past year?
    (c) What effect does such *koinonia* have on other people?
    (d) What links, if any, has your congregation with other congregations or with Christians outside your country?
12. What would you reply to someone who said: 'Christians talk a lot about "fellowship". But many other groups of people, both religious and non-religious, have fellowship with each other that is equally strong and effective.'?
    Do you think that Christians can learn about fellowship from other groups?
    In what ways do members of your own Church chiefly have fellowship with each other?

13. 'Day of Jesus Christ' (1.6).
    (a) How often do preachers preach about 'the day' and about Jesus's Coming? If often, why? If not often, why?
    (b) What do they say about it? How far is it good news?
    (c) Are people confusing the 'day of Jesus' with the day which could occur if nuclear weapons destroy the earth? What could you say to people who do confuse the two?
14. 'To feel thus about you all' (1.7). Paul seems to have been both the Philippians' friend and a person in authority over them. How far is it possible for someone in authority over you to be your friend?

1.9–11
Growth in Loving

INTRODUCTION

As Paul thought about the Christians at Philippi, he longed for them to become a stronger and a better congregation. They needed, for instance, to be more understanding in the way they looked after each other.

But he did not condemn or criticize them: he prayed for them, and then told them (in this passage) what his prayer had been about.

NOTES AND INTERPRETATION

My prayer (v. 9a): The word used for 'prayer' is studied under 4.6; here we shall consider prayer for other people (which Paul talked about in v. 9).

1. People sometimes say, 'God helps me if I pray to Him. I know this. But does He really help *other* people if I pray for them?' We may understand prayers for other people ('intercession') if we remember two truths:

(a) The human family is one family. What one human being does has a result for all other humans. Evil intention here can bring evil elsewhere: good intention here can bring good elsewhere too. If people explode a nuclear bomb in North Africa, radio-active dust (Strontium 90) from the explosion is blown away by the wind, and can poison the milk in India. That is an evil result. But it is equally true that if other people meet to pray, their prayer can also have a result for men and women living 2,000 miles away, but this time it will be a good result.

(b) God expects us to work with Him. We are 'God's fellow-workers' (1 Cor. 3.9 NEB). He offers His help and His healing at all times, but we cannot receive them unless we co-operate with Him.

Jesus offered to heal a man with a diseased arm, but the healing did not take place till the man 'co-operated' by stretching out his hand (Mark 3.5). So when one member of the human family is in trouble, either he himself or some other human being must do the work of co-operating with God; and prayer is one way of co-operating. The Philippian Christians needed God's help: they needed help in the way they treated other Church members. Someone had to co-operate with God and do the work of praying for them. Paul, on behalf of the human family, did this work, because he loved them.

2. What should we ask for? In all praying it is good to share everything with God, so naturally we share our hopes and fears for other people with Him. But praying for others is not telling God what they need. He knows what they most need. Our praying for them becomes: 'Lord, accept my love for them and give them whatever is best for them. Your will be done.'

3. Who can we pray for? It is probably easier to pray for members of our own family or our own nation, or for people we like. But as we become mature we see that we must offer prayer for everyone who is in need.

This is difficult because there are so many people in need that we have to choose for whom especially we shall pray. One man uses a daily newspaper to show him some of the people who need to be prayed for. Many Christians keep a notebook and under each day of the month they list the names of those for whom they will pray that day.

Your love may abound more and more (v. 9b): It was important that Christians at Philippi should more and more love each other so that they might be a united congregation. We see (e.g. in 2.2; 2.14) that there was division and complaining in the congregation.

Abound i.e. increase: Our lives are full of 'increases.' Parents may hope for an increase in the number of their children. Workers may hope for an increase in wages. Students hope for an increase in their understanding of a subject. Little children want to increase the number of words they can read. Paul says here, 'This is the place where increase is most needed – in loving!' The man who increases in other ways but not in loving is a poor man. The congregation that increases its income but not its care for strangers or its understanding of the Bible is a poor congregation.

Love: This translates the Greek word '*agape*' (which we find also in 1.16; 2.1; and 2.2). We see from 1 Corinthians 13.4–7 some ways in which we can tell that someone has '*agape*': he willingly accepts the trouble that other people give him ('patient' v. 4); he does what he can

20

to meet other people's needs ('kind' v. 4); he is happy when other people have some good thing that he himself does not have ('not jealous' v. 4); he draws attention to the goodness and achievements of other people ('not boastful' v. 4); he listens to other people's opinions carefully ('not arrogant' v. 5); he does his best to know what other people's feelings are ('not rude' v. 5); he can see the Spirit of God at work in others ('not insist on his own way' v. 5); he can accept what others give him, including criticism ('not irritable' v. 5); he can forgive those who have injured him ('not resentful' v. 5); he suffers pain when others do wrong ('not rejoice at wrong' v. 6); he is happy when others do right ('rejoices in the right' v. 6); he goes on loving under all circumstances ('bears . . . all things' v. 7).

The meaning of the word '*agape*' is different from that of three other Greek words also translated 'love', with which it is often confused: '*eros*' (love between a man and a woman), '*philia*' (friendship between people who like the same things), and '*storge*' (love between members of the same family).

Perfect '*agape*' has only been seen in the life of Jesus. 1 Corinthians 13 is really Paul's description of the way Jesus treated other people.

If we 'love', it is because the Spirit of Jesus has been given to us. 'We love, because he first loved us' (1 John 4.19). New Testament writers use the same word for God's love for us, for our love for Him, for our love for one another, and for our love for ourselves.

Love . . . with knowledge and all discernment (v. 9c): If we really 'love' a person we take the trouble to discover and understand ('discern') what that person most needs. If a beggar comes to the house we may give him money and food, with good intentions. But our love is without knowledge and understanding if it leads the beggar to remain a beggar, or prevents him from finding work and from gaining respect for himself.

When parents love their children with understanding they treat them in such a way that the children grow in responsibility and independence.

At one time in a district in Brazil two babies were dying out of every three that were born. To help them, a group of European Christians came and built a large hospital. They were so successful that in a short time nearly all the babies who were born lived and grew up, and the population grew rapidly. But there was not enough food to feed them all, and in the end there was starvation. If those Christians had loved with more 'understanding', they would surely have studied conditions in that country very carefully before planning what sorts of action they should take.

A group of young Christians in Sweden in 1962 heard about the needs of a district in North India. They travelled to the place and worked there with great vigour and good will. But their work failed. They bought land for farming at twice the normal price, and then found that it could not produce the crops that were needed. They found that the local doctor was cheating the people by charging huge fees for injections, but when they made this known, the doctor went somewhere else, and the district had no doctor at all. They persuaded the people of one town to give money and work to build better roads and drains, but only the rich people's roads were improved, and the gap between the rich and the poor was increased. Some of the Swedes said, 'It is no use caring for these people.' But their leader said, 'We cared for them without knowledge. Now we shall learn from our mistakes.'

Christians too often love with their feelings alone, and without careful thought, as if they expect God to produce good results in a magical way.

Approve what is excellent (v. 10): The Greek word here translated 'approve' means 'test'. (A shopkeeper sometimes tests a coin to see if it is real or false.) The word here translated 'excellent' means the things that are 'most important in life'. So Paul was telling his readers to make choices in the way they lived, and not always to accept the old ways. They were to ask, 'What matters more than anything else in our congregation?'

Every congregation needs to ask this. A group of English Christians spent a whole day discussing that one question, and answered, 'It matters most that we love and trust one another and welcome strangers as if they were Christ. It matters less that the church building is well decorated and that all members have paid their contributions.'

Every nation needs to ask the same question. For example, 'Which is more important, a few big factories that increase our overseas trade but employ few people, or a large number of small industries so that many are employed?.'

Pure and blameless (v. 10): 'Blameless' does not here mean 'perfect'; it means 'not causing other people to stumble'. What Paul meant was this: 'Remember that by your behaviour you either attract people to follow Christ or you make it difficult for them to do so. If you are dishonest or unforgiving, you are giving people good reasons for not joining the Church. Why should anyone want to become a Christian unless he finds that members of the Christian Church are honest and forgiving people?' See 1 Corinthians 10.31, 32: 'Do all to the glory of God. Give no offence to Jews or to Greeks.'

To the glory and praise of God (v. 11): Why did Paul want the congregation at Philippi to 'grow in loving'? It was in order that God might be praised and loved. That is what Christians are for.

For 'glory' see note on 4.20.

At a Student Conference, members studied these verses and then used them in a final act of worship, in the following way:

Leader: May we grow in our love for one another.
All: That God may be glorified and praised!
Leader: May our love be with understanding.
All: That God may be glorified and praised!
Leader: May we know what matters most in life.
All: That God may be glorified and praised!
Leader: May we be sincere in our dealings with others.
All: That God may be glorified and praised!
Leader: May our lives not be a stumbling block to the faith of others.
All: That God may be glorified and praised!
Leader: May we be open to receive those gifts which God offers through Jesus.
All: That God may be glorified and praised. Amen!

STUDY SUGGESTIONS

WORDS

1. What do you understand by the phrase 'co-operating with God'?
2. (a) How has the word 'Love' (v. 9) been translated into another language which you know? What is the full meaning of that word? How good a translation is it?
   (b) Which 5 of the following words would you use to describe the sort of love for which Paul used the Greek word *agape*?
   patient   passionate   caring   long-suffering   demanding
   partial   forgiving   sustaining   capricious
3. Which of the following words have the same or nearly the same meaning as 'abound' in v. 9?
   increase   bind   augment   be abundant   be limited   grow
   jump about

CONTENT

4. For what reason did Paul pray that the Philippians should 'grow in loving'?
5. What two truths can specially help us to understand the work of intercession, or praying for other people?
6. What did Paul mean when he told the Philippians to 'approve what is excellent'?

BIBLE,

7. In vv 9–11 Paul said that he prayed to God to give the Philippians special gifts. Put into your own words the gifts which Paul referred to.
8. Say in each of the following passages (i) Who Jesus was praying for; (ii) What He was asking God to do.
   (a) Luke 22.32   (b) Luke 23.34   (c) John 14.8–16
   (d) John 17.9–11   (e) John 17.20

DISCUSSION AND RESEARCH

9. 'My prayer' (v. 9). Compare your own prayers for other people with Paul's prayer for the Philippians in vv 9–11 (see no. 7 above). When you yourself pray to God for your friends, what do you ask Him for?
10. (a) Why is it important that Christians should love 'with know-ledge and all discernment' (i.e. with understanding)?
    (b) Read again the description on p. 21 of Christians failing to help people in Brazil with understanding. What do you think they should have done?
    (c) Give some other example of what can happen when people love and take loving action without understanding.
11. A student once said: 'God's love (*agape*) for us is so great that it includes every other sort of loving.' Do you agree? Give your reasons.
12. What is it that chiefly enables people to 'grow' in loving?
13. 'What matters more than anything else in a congregation?' (p. 22). If a group from your own Church met to discuss this question, what do you think their answer would be?
14. 'Blameless' means 'not causing other people to stumble' (p. 22). In what chief ways do you think that (a) the Churches in your country, (b) your own congregation, (c) you yourself, are perhaps causing those outside the Church to 'stumble', and making it less probable that they will want to join the Church?
15. 'Many Christians keep a notebook and . . . list the names of those for whom they will pray' (p. 20). One student said: 'If I did that I should feel like a "praying machine", not a loving person.' What are your own feelings on the subject?

1.12–18
God Makes Use of Opposition

INTRODUCTION

When Christians hear of other members of the Church suffering because they are Christians they feel it is difficult to bear. It was difficult for the Philippians to bear that Paul, their founder, was in prison, and to be without news of him. It was also puzzling, just as Jesus's disciples had been puzzled when He said that He 'must suffer' (Mark 8.31). See also 1 Peter 4.12: 'Do not be surprised at the fiery ordeal . . . as though something strange were happening.'

So Paul wrote to tell them his news. Above all he assured them that the gospel was being preached. This is the chief message of the whole section vv 12–26. God was using Paul's imprisonment, he said, in two ways:

1. Those who were not Christians had had to take notice of the gospel (see v. 13). The soldiers who were guarding Paul asked, 'Who are these Christians? Why is this man in prison? Who is this Jesus whom Paul serves? What makes him go to prison for Jesus's sake?' And Paul the prisoner was free to tell them.

2. The news that the gospel was being preached in this way was encouraging other Christians. They were becoming 'confident in the Lord' (v. 14).

Some readers ask questions about Paul's imprisonment: Where was it? Was he locked up in a prison, or chained to a guard, or was he 'under house-arrest'? Which praetorian guard was responsible for him? Paul did not give the answers in these verses. What he has done is more important: he has shared with his readers his firm belief that even in very difficult circumstances Christians can continue to serve Christ, and can tell the world about Him (v. 18), because they are strengthened by God's power.

NOTES AND INTERPRETATION

Brethren (v. 12): Compare 'partnership' (v. 5). Paul was the Philippians' leader, but he also saw himself as their 'brother'.

New Testament writers used the word 'brotherliness' to describe the fellowship that existed among Christians between leaders and led, employers and employed, masters and slaves, Jews and non-Jews, because each served the same Lord. So they could speak freely to one another.

Not all Church leaders have behaved like the brothers of those whom they led. Sometimes they have been more like army commanders. Paul himself sometimes seemed more like a school teacher than a brother, e.g. in 2 Corinthians 13.2: 'I warned those who sinned before . . . and warn them now . . . if I come again I will not spare them.'

What has happened to me has really served to advance the gospel (v. 12): What has happened: These words refer to the pain of imprisonment which Paul was suffering.

Concerning this suffering, we note:

(a) Although men and women suffer imprisonment for different reasons (e.g. some are political prisoners, other criminals, others 'prisoners of conscience'), there is suffering which all prisoners share and which Paul shared. Being a great Christian leader did not prevent Paul's sufferings from being real.

(b) Paul was in prison because of his beliefs. In this way he shared the experience of the thousands who are in prison as we read this, and many of whom are tortured because of what they believe. We think of the very many Roman Catholics in South America who are in prison without a trial; of Pavel Solovyov, aged 38, sentenced to three years imprisonment in the USSR for singing hymns in a public park; Leonidas Tsaouis, aged 21, serving a four-year sentence for refusing, on religious grounds, to serve in the Greek army; Kenneth Matiba, former government minister in Kenya, who was imprisoned (without charge) for supporting a multi-party system; Ma Theigee, an art teacher and member of the National League for Democracy in Myanmar (Burma), who has been arrested, tried by a military court, and is in solitary confinement, but with no charges against her.

(c) Paul was imprisoned because of his belief in Jesus. He did not suffer more than other Christians, but he represents all who have endured suffering for the sake of Christ.

(d) Although Paul's sufferings were as real as those of other prisoners, he received strength from outside himself (like many Christians since). For example, the Philippians supported him by their fellowship (1.7) and, even more, he was strengthened by knowing that God would one day triumph over all evil (3.21). This is the reason why he could say that God was actually using his suffering.

To advance the gospel: Paul's imprisonment had not hindered the preaching of the gospel: it had actually helped it. This had not happened by chance, but because Paul had let God make use of the event.

'What has happened to me has really served to advance the gospel' (1.12). 'There does not seem to be any situation, however bad, which God cannot redeem' (p. 28).

This picture shows John Bunyan, a Baptist minister who was imprisoned in 1660 for preaching, which at that time was illegal for Nonconformists in England. He let God 'redeem' the twelve years he spent in prison, and he used it to write the *Pilgrim's Progress* and other religious books. What attitude of mind do you think made it possible for him to do this? What attitude would have made it impossible?

Because God is creator and re-creator, there are always times when He can use what seems to be useless. There are many examples of this.

In God's world what some people regard as 'rubbish' can become compost, and milk that some housewives would throw away as 'sour' can become cheese.

Paul's imprisonment in Philippi became the time when the jailer and his family were baptized. (see Acts 16.16–34) It was this sort of event that led Paul to write, 'when I am weak, then I am strong' (2 Cor. 12.10).

According to Genesis 45, this is how Joseph interpreted his slavery in Egypt. He said to his brothers, 'God sent me before you to preserve life (v. 5) . . . it was not you who sent me here' (v. 8).

The worst thing that has ever been done by human beings was the killing of Jesus, yet under God it became the best thing that ever happened. 'This is the stone which was rejected . . . but which has become the head of the corner' (Acts 4.11).

Samuel Ajayi Crowther, the first Nigerian Church leader, travelled from Freetown to Lagos in 1850, and prepared to travel and preach over a wide area. Owing to war, he could not move from the coast for eighteen months. Instead of complaining of 'disaster', he used the opportunity to translate large parts of the Bible into Yoruba.

A hundred years later, a Christian nurse in North India was murdered by a young man who had a complaint against the hospital where she worked. Her funeral was a time for such joyful thanksgiving for her life that Hindu friends began to take the gospel seriously for the first time.

In all these events we cannot say that God 'sent' the pain or the suffering or the disappointment. What God did was to 'redeem' it, i.e. turn it into an opportunity for good. There does not seem to be any situation, however bad, which God cannot 'redeem'.

It has become known throughout the whole Praetorian guard (1.13): This verse is important because in it we see how marvellously God 'used' or 'redeemed' Paul's imprisonment.

But readers may also ask, 'Which guard was it?' In other words, 'From where did Paul write this letter?'

1. It is likely that he wrote it from Rome in AD 62, because:

(a) We think of Rome rather than any other city when we read of 'the whole Praetorian guard' and (in 4.22) 'those of Caesar's household'.

(b) We know from Acts 28.30, 31 that Paul was imprisoned for at least two years in Rome.

(c) Paul needed help in prison (from Timothy and Epaphroditus), and Rome was a place where he would need help, because the Church there was small and weak.

2. But some scholars think that Paul wrote from Ephesus between AD 54 and 57. They say:

(a) Paul said in Philippians 1.1 that Timothy was with him, and according to Acts 19.22 it was at Ephesus that Timothy was with Paul.

(b) Paul could have been referring to Roman guards in Ephesus when he wrote Philippians 1.13 and 4.22.

(c) During Paul's two years' imprisonment messengers made at least four journeys between Philippi and Paul's prison. If he was in prison in Ephesus there was plenty of time in which they could make these journeys, because Ephesus is near Philippi. But Rome is 1200 kms by sea from Philippi, and it is not certain if there was time for such journeys to take place.

3. Others believe that Paul wrote from Caesarea (in AD 59), mainly because we know from Acts 23.35 and 24.27 that Paul was imprisoned there.

From these various answers which scholars give to the question 'Where did Paul write this letter?' we see that no one is sure what the true answer is. Usually we are better able to interpret a letter if we know where the writer was when he wrote it. But in the case of the letter to the Philippians the way we interpret it does not depend at all on our knowing where it was written.

Preach Christ (v. 15): In v. 14 Paul had referred to 'speaking' the word of God (i.e. the gospel). In vv 15–18 he used two other words, 'preach' and 'proclaim' which he used very often in his letters. These two words mean almost the same thing.

'Preaching' (or 'proclaiming') does not mean standing up on a raised platform and delivering a sermon in a church service. It means making the gospel known at any time and in any place, in such a way that non-Christians as well as Christians can believe that it is good news for them.

A preacher is anyone who says something like the following:

(a) 'Something has happened', e.g. God has raised up Jesus (Acts 2.24; 3.15), and I have come to share the news and to tell you the story.

(b) 'Taking this news seriously has made a difference to my life' (Acts 4.13: 'When they saw the boldness of Peter and John . . . they recognized that they had been with Jesus').

(c) 'Test this for yourselves' (Acts 3.19: 'Repent . . . and turn again').

There are, of course, times when a Christian leader must give 'teaching', for example on how to live the Christian life, how to be a member of the Church, etc. But this 'teaching' is not the same as 'preaching' or 'proclaiming'.

A congregation is healthy when its leaders and members are engaged in 'preaching and proclaiming' and also in 'teaching'.

Some preach Christ from envy and rivalry (v. 15): Who were these
'preachers'? They were not preachers of false beliefs. They were not
the same as those to whom Paul referred in Galatians 3.1, who were
persuading others to return to the old Jewish way of thinking about
God. If they had been, Paul would have written about them in the
same way: 'Who has bewitched you?' As it was, Paul could 'rejoice'
that they were preaching (v. 18).

Probably they were leading members of the Church in Philippi, who
had been there before Paul first arrived and who were unhappy that he
was now being treated as more important than they were. So although
they preached a Christian message ('Christ is proclaimed' v. 18), they
were envious of Paul. They regarded him more as a rival than as a
partner (v. 15). As a result, instead of *koinonia* or togetherness there
was a split between them and Paul ('partisanship' v. 17), and this was
painful to him ('afflict me' v. 17).

This can happen between Christians today. Church workers do
sometimes envy or fear or dislike one another. It happens because they
are sinful human beings. It may also be because they come from
different backgrounds with different customs, and for other reasons.
As Paul said, 'We have this treasure in earthen vessels' (2 Cor. 4.7).
Paul himself was of course not without his faults, and he was not an
easy person to work with (see 2 Cor. 2.1–4; Gal. 2.11–14).

But, as Paul showed in v. 18, we should not resign from Christian
work merely because we find other Christians difficult, or because we
disapprove of their way of doing their work. The Church must make
known the gospel by word and deed, and this does not happen unless
members are allowing other members to do it in the way those others
think best. Compare Mark 9.38–39: 'John said . . . "Teacher, we saw
a man casting out demons in your name, and we forbade him because
he was not following us." But Jesus said, "Do not forbid him".'

STUDY SUGGESTIONS

WORDS

1. 'Teaching' is not the same as 'preaching' or 'proclaiming' (p. 29).
   Which of the following words mean 'teaching' and which mean
   'preaching'?
   guiding declaring instructing training announcing witnessing
   explaining challenging
2. For each of the following three words, write a sentence to show its
   meaning, and also the difference between its meaning and the
   meaning of each of the other two.
   partisanship partnership participation

CONTENT

3. Paul called the Philippians 'brethren' (v. 12). What does this tell us about the relationship between Christians in those times?
4. What did Paul mean when he said that 'some preach Christ from envy and rivalry' (v. 15)?
5. In what ways did Paul's imprisonment 'serve to advance the gospel' (v. 12)?

BIBLE

6. According to each of the following verses, (i) Who was 'preaching' (v. 15)? and (ii) What was their message?
   (a) Matt. 4.17 (b) Acts 4.2 (c) Acts 8.35 (d) Acts 17.18
   (e) 1 Cor. 1.23
7. 'The pain of imprisonment which Paul was suffering' (p. 26). What sort of suffering did Paul experience, according to each of the following verses?
   (a) 1.7 (b) 1.8 (c) 1.15 (d) 2.17 (e) 2.27 (f) 3.18
   (g) 4.12

DISCUSSION AND RESEARCH

8. 'Even in very difficult circumstances Christians can continue to serve Christ because they are strengthened by God's power' (p. 25).
   Give two examples from the history of the Church, of Christians who were able to serve Christ in difficult circumstances.
9. 'God can use what seems to be useless' – 'rubbish' can become compost and 'sour' milk can become cheese (p. 28).
   Give some other examples of ways in which God 'works for good' (Rom. 8.28) by using what seems to be useless.
10. 'Instead of togetherness there was a split' (p. 30).
    What are some of the most likely causes of a 'split' in any Christian congregation, and how can they be overcome?
11. Which do you think it is more important for a Church Leader to do, 'preaching' or 'teaching'? Give reasons for your answer.
12. 'What has happened to me' (1.12) i.e. imprisonment.
    (a) What do you think is the most painful part of being a prisoner?
    (b) What effect does imprisonment have on prisoners? What effect did it have on Paul?
13. 'Preach' (v. 15). A woman went to see the headmaster of the school where her son attended because the son had been getting into trouble. She said afterwards, 'He didn't listen to my questions. He just preached at me.' What is the difference between this headmaster's 'preaching' and the sort of preaching referred to in v. 16?

14. 'Whether in pretence or in truth . . .' (1.18).
   (a) When you yourself think that other Christians are working with wrong motives, how do you behave towards them?
   (b) How do you know what is the right thing to do in such circumstances?

1.19–26

Ready to Live, Ready to Die

INTRODUCTION

The language of this part of Paul's letter is not simple, because he was trying to share his experience of 'being pushed two directions' (v. 23a), and because he was using the language of a lover or a poet rather than ordinary phrases, e.g. 'to live is Christ' (v. 21).

His main thoughts were:

1. I believe that God will 'deliver' me (v. 19 and vv 25, 26).

2. Whether I shall go on living in this world or whether they will kill me, I shall gladly accept either (v. 20).

3. I can say this because for me all living, whether it is living here in this world or living beyond the grave, is in Christ and with Christ (v. 21a).

4. But I still have a problem: which should I ask God for, life or death? (vv 22–24).

What we chiefly notice here is the way in which Paul, while being in a state of great uncertainty, showed a calm and steady acceptance of whatever should happen to him.

NOTES AND INTERPRETATION

Through your prayers (v. 19a): In his imprisonment Paul needed support, and in this verse said that he was getting support from two sources: the prayers of the Christians and 'the Spirit of Jesus Christ' (see note below).

How is it that the prayers of one person can make a difference to others? It is because such prayers are a way of co-operating with God (see note on 1.9). God wishes to do His work through His body, the Church, and part of His strengthening of those in need is given through the prayers of others. This is why we can say that prayer changes things.

We may add that those who are in need are also strengthened by knowing that someone is praying for them. A few years ago a group of soldiers were captured by the enemy and were kept in harsh conditions for over a year. Many of them gave up hope and died. Of those who survived, and were eventually released, a large number said they were alive because they knew that people at home were praying for them.

Paul said in several of his letters that he depended on the prayers of other Christians. See 2 Corinthians 1.11: 'You also must help us by prayer, so that many will give thanks on our behalf.' And 'I appeal to you, brethren . . . to strive together with me in your prayers to God on my behalf, that I may be delivered . . . so that by God's will I may come to you with joy' (Rom. 15.30–32).

The help of the Spirit of Jesus Christ (v. 19b): Some people say that this means the Holy Spirit which *is* Jesus, as in Acts 16.7; 2 Corinthians 3.17: 'Now the Lord is the Spirit'. Others think that it means the Holy Spirit which was *in* Jesus, as in John 1.32: 'I saw the Spirit descend . . . and it remained on him.' We cannot know which Paul had in mind. What mattered for him was that in his sufferings he could depend on more than human help, he could depend on the very same Spirit of God which filled Jesus Himself.

This will turn out for my deliverance (v. 19c): What sort of deliverance did Paul mean here? The Greek word is usually translated 'salvation' (see note on 2.12). Clearly he did not mean 'release from prison', because in v. 20 he said that he might soon die.

Some interpret it as 'salvation from eternal spiritual destruction' as in 1.28.

Probably Paul meant deliverance from faithlessness and cowardice during his whole work for Christ, i.e. 'deliverance from being judged guilty in what I am doing'. This is the meaning of the word in Job 13.16, (where the RSV translation is 'salvation') which Paul may have been quoting.

It is my eager expectation and hope (v. 20): 'Eager expectation' means 'stretching out one's neck to see what lies ahead'. 'Hope' is one of the great words of the New Testament:

1. Hope is confidence in God's love and power. Thus it is different from a cheerful outlook or careful calculations. See 2.19: 'I hope in the Lord Jesus.'

2. Hope is confidence in God as regards the future. (The word 'faith' e.g. in v. 25 refers to confidence in God as regards the past and present.) The future includes the rest of our lives in this world, our life to come after death, and the completion of God's whole creation (Rom. 8.18–25).

3. Hope is based on what God has done. See 1 Peter 1.3: 'We have been born anew to a living hope through the resurrection of Jesus Christ'.

4. Hope is kept alive by our being in touch with the living God. See Romans 5.5: 'Hope does not disappoint us, because God's love has been poured into our hearts.'

With full courage . . . Christ will be honoured (v. 20): The word translated 'full courage' means 'speaking freely' (which no one can do unless he has courage).

Christ will be honoured in my body, whether by life or by death (v. 20): The NEB has: 'The greatness of Christ will shine out in my person, whether through my life or through my death.'

Paul compared his life to a public exhibition, in which passers-by could see the glory of Christ.

We see in this whole phrase the way in which Paul was ready to accept anything, including life or death, which would lead others to honour Jesus Christ.

In what ways can Christians 'accept' life?

1. They do not do it by giving up hope, or by ceasing to care what happens, or by pretending that they do not care. That is not 'accepting'.

2. They do it by living the words, 'Your will be done', and by committing themselves into God's hands, and by depending on Him rather than on circumstances. See notes on 4.4; 4.6; 4.11, 12, 13.

3. They are therefore ready for both pleasant and painful events. If pleasant, a Christian gives thanks rather than boasting. If painful, he increases his dependence on God rather than complaining.

4. They continue to avoid pain, if this is possible, and to fight injustice where it exists. 'Doing nothing' is not accepting.

5. They can accept life because Jesus came into our world and accepted life as we live it. Before Christ, sufferers either endured their pain, or did nothing except complain and question (like Job in some parts of that book). But when Jesus had come people saw that God was sharing the sufferings and deaths of mankind, and they could therefore say, 'If pain comes, I will somehow use it as a way of sharing His sufferings and giving Him honour.' See also notes on 4.11, 12, 13.

To live is Christ (v. 21a): As a Jew, Paul had served God since his birth, but it was God-as-shown-forth-in-Christ who had given him what he most valued in life. Whichever way he turned, there was Christ! Christ had changed the direction of Paul's life, had set him on a new way – had given him his life's work and the strength to do it. Paul had found his true self in Christ. Above all, Christ had given him His own fellowship.

To 'live is Christ' was a powerful way of saying what Paul often said about 'living *in* Christ'. See note on 4.10.

We are reminded of St Patrick's hymn (written in the 5th century AD):

'Christ will be honoured in my body, whether by life or by death' (1.20).

Archbishop Oscar Romero was killed in El Salvador in March 1980 (see pp. 71, 72). How far is it true to say that by his death he led others to 'honour Christ'? Or could he have achieved more by other means?

Christ be with me, Christ within me,
Christ behind me, Christ before me,
Christ beside me, Christ to win me,
Christ to comfort and restore me,
Christ beneath me, Christ above me,
Christ in quiet, Christ in danger,
Christ in hearts of all that love me,
Christ in mouth of friend and stranger.

Paul expressed the same thoughts more fully in 3.7–14.

To die is gain (v. 21b): Alongside these words, we should also study v. 23b, 'To depart and be with Christ, for that is far better' (see note on that verse).

How was it possible for Paul to hold such beliefs? No Old Testament writer had ever said this, e.g. see Isaiah 38.18: 'Sheol cannot thank thee, death cannot praise thee.' The great philosopher Socrates did not believe it either. He said, 'The hour of my departure has arrived, and we go our ways, I to die, you to live. Which is better only the gods know.'

Paul could say it because Christ had come and had died and had been raised to life. As a result he and other New Testament writers held ideas about death of the body such as the following. They thought of death:

(a) As '*being*' with Christ (as in 23b);

(b) As a *deepening* of relationship with Christ. (See Rom. 6.8: 'if we have died with Christ, we believe that we shall also live with him.');

(c) As a *release* from the limits which we experience in this life. (2 Cor. 5.8:'We would rather be away from the body and at home with the Lord');

(d) As a sort of peaceful *sleeping* (1 Thess. 4.13);

(e) As an *entrusting* of life into God's hands (see Luke 23.46);

(f) As a *completion* of this life (John 19.30: 'It is accomplished!' NEB).

Those who see death in this way and accept it have peace of mind. Those who refuse to think or speak about it are pretending that it will not happen. (This does not mean that we should think about it continually; that is a disease of the mind.)

No wise person pretends to know what happens after death. Those who wrote the words referred to above, and those who today speak about life after death, do so in hope. They have hope because of what they already know of the love and power of God.

Note: In vv 20 and 21 Paul was referring to the death of the body, but some New Testament writers, especially John, use the word 'death' in a different way. In John 5.24; 6.50; 11.25, 26, for example, death means the result of a person's sin, e.g. the pain of knowing that he is separated from God. (It does not seem to refer to the destruction of his soul.)

If it is to be life in the flesh, that means fruitful labour for me (v. 22): i.e.: 'If I am to go on living in this world, then I can go on doing useful work.' (Paul's actual words were: 'If living in flesh this to me fruit of work.' Did he perhaps scribble these words down as a private note and forget to write it out fully later?) See note on 4.19.

As Paul used the word which is translated 'flesh', it is important to note the different meanings which writers in the Bible give it:

(a) Life on earth, human beings using their bodies, minds and spirits in this world. This is its meaning in this verse and in John 1.14.

(b) The limited powers and 'weakness' of life on earth, e.g. in Isaiah 40.6: 'All flesh is grass, and all its beauty is like the flower of the field . . .'

(c) All of a person's life on earth which is not under the control of God's Spirit. 'Flesh' thus means any thinking or worshipping, any service to our neighbours, any activity at all which we fail to do in dependence on God and under His authority. See Philippians 3.4 and Romans 7.5: 'While we were living in the flesh, our sinful passions . . . were at work'.

Note: Writers in the Bible do *not* teach that a person's physical body is evil and that on the contrary his spirit is good. Some Eastern religions have taught this. Some Christians also have followed them, teaching for example that it is wicked to enjoy the flesh in sexual intercourse but good to enjoy spiritual conversation. But we do not find such teaching in the Gospels or in Paul's letters.

I am hard pressed between the two (v. 23a): This is picture-language. It could be a picture of a traveller in a deep valley who can see no way out. On one side is the steep mountain of 'life', on the other the equally steep mountain of 'death'. Both sides seem to be pressing down upon him. Or could it be a picture of a voter in an election, with members of opposite parties pulling him in different directions.

The same picture-language was used by Jesus, 'There is a baptism I must undergo, and how "strained" I am, till it is over' (Luke 12.50, Phillips).

The two directions in which Paul was being pushed are referred to in v. 23b and v. 24.

Being 'pushed in two directions' is very often a part of the suffering which Christians have been told to expect. A man is offered a new job, and his wife advises him in one way, his business partners advise him differently. The German Dietrich Bonhoeffer was teaching theology in the USA in 1940 while Hitler was in control of Germany. Some theologians begged him to stay in the USA, some Germans begged him to return to Germany, although at risk of his life. (With the agreement of his wife he did return, and was executed just before the war ended.)

My desire is to depart and be with Christ (v. 23b): The Greek word translated 'depart' is another picture-word. It can refer to pulling up tent-pegs after camping, or releasing a boat from its anchor as it sets out to sea.

'To be with Christ' shows that Paul believed that after death he would have fellowship with Christ. This fellowship would be even closer than the fellowship he had by being 'in Christ' on earth. (See 1 Thess. 4.16, 17 and note on 2.19.)

This belief in fellowship with Christ after death seems at first sight different from two other ways in which Christians sometimes refer to life after death:

1. That there is sleep from which we shall at the end be woken. See 1 Thessalonians 4.13: 'We would not have you ignorant concerning those who are asleep.'

2. That we are taken through stages of training and purifying before being brought into the presence of Christ. See John 14.2, where the word translated 'rooms' means stopping-places on a long journey. Paul himself may have regarded existence after death as a time of purifying, if that is the right way to interpret 1 Corinthians 3.12–15: 'Each man's work will become manifest . . . the fire will test what sort of work each one has done' (v. 13).

But it is not necessary to see these ideas as contradicting each other. After all, it 'does not yet appear what we shall be' (1 John 3.2). In none of those passages did the writer claim to 'describe' life after death.

I shall . . . continue with you all, for your progress and joy in the faith (v. 25): Although Paul had said earlier that he did not know what would happen to him (and repeated this in 2.17), he added here 'I believe I shall be with you again, in order that you may make progress in your faith and have joy in it', and repeated his hope in v. 26. It is possible that Paul did see the Christians of Philippi again, but we do not know.

The word translated 'continue with' means 'remain beside someone who needs you', just as God's Holy Spirit is called '*Paraclete*', the one who is 'called in to stand beside' us. See John 14.16 (Phillips) and Phil. 2.1a.

'Progress' is an idea which Paul often used to describe a healthy congregation (see 1 Thess. 4.1; 'more and more'). A congregation needs to ask itself from time to time not only: 'Are we maintaining what we have received?', but also: 'In what ways are we developing it to meet the needs of the present time?'

For the meaning of 'all' see note on 1.4; for 'joy' see note on 4.4.
That in me you may have ample cause to glory in Christ Jesus, because of my coming to you again (v. 26): that is: 'when I visit you again you will be able to see in me what Jesus Christ can do for a follower of His, and will give Him the 'glory'. The word translated 'glory' here is sometimes translated 'boast about' (see note on 3.3).

STUDY SUGGESTIONS

WORDS

1. 'This will turn out for my deliverance' (v. 19).
   Which of the following sorts of 'deliverance' did Paul *not* mean?
   (a) getting rid of something unpleasant (b) being carried from one place to another (c) being set free from one's own bad qualities (d) being released from captivity (e) being saved from physical danger
2. (a) What is your understanding of the word 'hope' as used by writers in the NT?
   (b) In what ways does its meaning in the NT differ from its meaning when it is used in ordinary conversation today?

CONTENT

3. From what two sources did Paul say that he was getting help and encouragement in his imprisonment?
4. How do we know what sort of 'deliverance' Paul was expecting?
5. In v. 21b Paul said 'To die is gain'.
   (a) What 'gain' did he believe that death would bring him?
   (b) What enabled him to hold this belief?
   (c) In what chief way did this belief differ from the belief about death held by writers of the OT?

BIBLE

6. 'The conflict which you saw to be mine' (v. 30). In what ways did Paul suffer in Philippi, according to Acts 16.19-24?
7. 'Ideas about death of the body' (p. 36). What ideas about death did the writers of the following passages have:
   (a) Psalm 6.5 (b) Isa. 38.18 (c) John 19.30 (d) Rom. 8.38
   (e) Phil. 1.23b (f) 2 Tim. 1.10 (g) Rev. 14.13
8. The word 'flesh' can mean (i) life on earth; (ii) life in its weakness; (iii) life which is not lived in obedience to God (p. 37). What is its meaning in each of the following passages?
   (a) John 1.14 (b) John 6.63 (c) Rom. 7.5 (d) Gal. 5.16
   (e) Col. 2.11

DISCUSSION AND RESEARCH

9. 'In his imprisonment Paul needed support' (p. 32). In which countries today are there Christians who are suffering imprisonment for their faith? In what ways can other Christians, including you yourself, give them the 'support' they need?
10. 'Christ will be honoured' (v. 20). What are some of the ways in which we can lead others to 'honour' Christ?
11. 'No wise person pretends to know what happens after death' (p. 36).
    (a) Discuss with one or two friends what each of you *really* believes about life after death.
    (b) How far do you share the ideas of NT writers as listed on p. 36.
    (c) Do you think that there will be further training or purifying after death?
    (d) What is the teaching of your own Church on this subject?
    (e) Find out what answers are given by other Churches in your area.
    (f) In what ways, if at all, is your belief different from what most non-Christians in your area believe?
12. 'Paul said that he was getting support from the prayers of the Christians' (p. 32). Give any examples you can from your own experience, of receiving 'support' from other people's prayers.
13. Do you think the congregation you belong to is (a) 'maintaining what it has received' and (b) 'developing it to meet the needs of the present time' (p. 38)? What more might it do in order to make progress in the faith? Is there anything more that you as an individual could do?

1.27–30

Stand Firm Together

INTRODUCTION

Here Paul was saying, 'Be united' (see note on v. 27 'one spirit'), and 'Be willing to suffer' (see note on v. 29).

Be united. These verses (27–30) are the beginning of a long section of this letter (1.27—2.18) throughout which Paul urged his readers to be united.

Why was it difficult for them to be united? We may notice two reasons (see also the Introduction to 2.1–4):

1. The various members of the congregation at Philippi, as happens in many city congregations in the world today, had belonged to different religions and came from different races (see note on 1.12). Naturally they held different opinions about how to live the gospel.

2. The Philippians were being persecuted. Often, when there is persecution, there are very different ideas, among those who are being persecuted, as to the right action to take. Those who resist very courageously may feel that they are superior to those who are afraid.

Be willing to suffer. The Philippians needed to be united because their opponents would attack them and cause them suffering. They must not be surprised at this, but accept it as Paul himself did (v. 30).

NOTES AND INTERPRETATION

Let your manner of life be worthy of the gospel (v. 27a): From the Greek word which is here translated 'your manner of life' we get our words 'politics' and 'polite'. It means living as a member of a community. As Philippi was a Roman colony, its inhabitants were proud of being Roman citizens. So Paul was saying, 'you are Roman citizens and therefore you behave in a way that suits Roman customs. But you are also Christians, therefore as you mix with others behave in a way that befits the gospel'.

We see from Paul's use of this word that Christians show their love for God, not in isolation from the rest of the world, but by the way in which they *relate* to other people. They relate to their fellow-citizens, and so, for example, they go to the wedding of a neighbour's daughter, and they pay their taxes, and they are concerned with their country's politics. They also relate to their fellow-Christians, and so they pray and work with them.

There are Christians who say, 'My religion is a matter between myself and my God.' Clearly they forget that the way they know and trust and join with other members of the congregation is part of being a Christian. Or they say, 'A truly spiritual Christian is not concerned with the affairs of the world.' But by saying this they are escaping from the duty to take part in the life of those amongst whom they live. They are escaping from Jesus's word to be 'salt to the world' (Matt. 5.13, NEB).

Worthy of the gospel: This does not mean that a Christian's behaviour can ever be sufficiently good or could ever *earn* God's approval. Paul had been urging the Philippians to be united. So here his meaning was, 'Let your behaviour fit the gospel which you preach. If you are not reconciled to one another, that does not fit the gospel in which Jesus preached reconciliation between God and human beings, and between one person and another.'

In one spirit, with one mind striving side by side for the faith of the gospel (v. 27b):

In one spirit: This phrase (along with 'with one mind' and 'side by side') refers to the Christian unity which the Philippians needed (see also note on 2.2). What is Christian unity?

(a) There is 'unity' when Christians who hold different ideas, or who perhaps do not even like each other, share a love for Jesus Christ, and have the same aims. 'Unity' does not mean holding the same ideas or liking the same things.

(b) Unity is necessary so that members can do the work that God intends the Church to do (see note on 1.5). How can non-Christians believe in Christ the Reconciler if they do not see His followers being reconciled to each other? Christians must be free from fighting against each other if they are to fight the evils which attack the Church (see note on 'striving' below).

(c) Unity is easily destroyed in a congregation, e.g. when members pay more attention to what they do than to the reasons for doing it, or more attention to which person is doing it than to what he does. When they are so keen on using some special music in worship, or some method of accountancy, but forget the reasons why the worship or the accountancy is done, there is disunity. See also 1 Corinthians 3.4–7, where we see that the Corinthians were divided because they paid more attention to the leaders of each 'party' in the congregation than they did to Christ Himself.

Striving side by side for the faith of the gospel:

(a) In this sentence Paul put many thoughts into a small space, and as a result the whole meaning is not very clear. See notes on 1.22 and 4.19. It probably means 'striving side by side to bring people to put their "faith" (i.e. confidence) in God, faith which they will have through hearing the gospel'.

But some think that the meaning is 'striving side by side against evil, supported by your confidence in the truth of the gospel'.

'Faith' nearly always means 'confidence in God' in the New Testament (see note on 3.9b). For 'gospel' see note on 1.5.

(b) It may be that when Paul wrote this he was thinking of a line of trained spearmen. If they kept side by side in a battle it was difficult for an enemy to overcome them. Philip of Macedon, after whom Philippi was named, had won many battles by the use of such spearmen, and the people of Philippi would have understood this sort of picture-language.

Or perhaps Paul was thinking of the Games, wrestling, and athletics of the Greeks. The word translated 'striving' really means 'being athletes together' (see 2 Tim. 2.5). For many people today football is the chief game and we might explain this section to them as: 'let me hear that your defence is firmly resisting the attacks of the other side . . . that you are playing together as a team (v. 27) . . . that you are not frightened by your opponents who are known to be a strong side. Then your courage will be a proof that they have no hope of winning . . . a sign to them of their collapse and of your victory (v. 28) . . . you are up against the same opponents against whom I have often played (v. 30).'

Whether Paul was thinking of battles or of games, it is clear that he saw living as a Christian as a struggle. In some Churches, when someone is baptized, the following words are said, 'I sign you with the sign of the cross, that you may not be ashamed to . . . fight against sin, the world, and the devil', e.g. against the temptations in yourselves, against the scorn of outsiders who attack the Church for being 'unpatriotic' or 'revolutionary', against governments that aim to destroy the Church.

If a Christian (or a congregation) is not engaged in some sort of struggle, it may be a sign that he is failing to follow Christ. An African bishop visiting Britain in 1980 said that English Christians seemed to be too contented. They reminded him of a sleeping lion. 'This', he said, 'is because they are following past heroes instead of Jesus Christ who is alive today.' Recently in Malaysia, where most people are Muslims, twenty-three Chinese Christians in a small congregation decided to become Muslims. Some of the other members lost hope and spoke of closing down their church, but the pastor said, 'Go out and find them and bring our old friends back!'

This is a clear omen to them of their destruction, but of your salvation (v. 28): That is, 'this, the confidence which you show and which is God's gift, will be a sure sign ("omen") to them that it is God Himself against whom they are fighting, and that their opposition to God will result in their destruction. But it is a sure sign that you are being saved.' Paul himself had experienced that when he was attacking Christians before his conversion, he was in fact attacking Jesus Himself (Acts 9.5).

It was also Gamaliel's experience, 'If this plan is of God . . . you might even be found opposing God!' (Acts 5.39).

For 'salvation' see note on 2.12.

Destruction: What sort of destruction was Paul writing about?

1. Perhaps he meant that some people have opposed God so often that He cannot give them a further chance to repent, so that their souls will be totally annihilated. See Matthew 10.28: 'Fear him who can destroy both soul and body in hell.' See also Revelation 20.14.

2. Perhaps he meant that such people will suffer the pain of 'permanent separation from God' rather than 'annihilation'. See Matthew 8.12: 'The sons of the kingdom will be thrown into the outer darkness'. See also Matthew 25.46.

3. Perhaps Paul was saying that although people's sinfulness leads to a painful loss of fellowship with God, His forgiveness is so permanent

that no one could ever be totally outside it. Like a shepherd He will 'go after the one which is lost, until he finds it' (Luke 15.4).

There has never been agreement among Christians as to the true interpretation of this verse. But there is firm agreement about the following important truths:

1. There is a real struggle between good and evil in the universe, and the Church must take part in it.

2. The way we live now has an effect on our existence in eternity.

3. Only God knows who is being 'saved' and who is not, and no truly 'saved' people appoint themselves as judge in this matter.

It has been granted to you that . . . you should suffer for His sake (v. 29): It has been granted: i.e. 'God, out of his generosity, has given you the honour . . .' The root of the word which is translated 'granted' means 'grace'. See 1.2; 1.7; 4.23.

Grace is:

(a) One person helping another person out of kindness, not because they owe the othe anything or expect a reward. (See Luke 6.33: 'If you do good to those who do good to you, what credit is that to you?') When a great Christian in Cairo died, someone said of him: 'He was truly gracious. He was the only man who kissed our babies when they were lying dead.'

(b) God's generosity in sending Jesus to live and die and rise again for us. This is what Paul usually means by 'grace' (see 2 Cor. 8.9: 'You know the grace of our Lord Jesus Christ, that . . . for your sake he became poor').

(c) God treating unworthy people far better than they deserve (see Rom. 12.3; 15.15; 1 Cor. 3.10; Gal. 2.9; also Eph. 2.8: 'For by grace you have been saved through faith, and this is not your own doing, it is the gift of God').

(d) God creating a relationship rather than giving a gift. Because of God's grace, Christians have become 'sons' of God (see Heb. 12.7).

You should . . . suffer for His sake: How can anyone regard it as a duty or an honour to suffer? How could Peter and the other apostles 'rejoice that they were counted worthy to suffer dishonour for the name' (Acts 5.41)?

The answer is two-fold:

1. By suffering willingly, Christians are sharing in God's own activity. God has treated us as 'sons', and sons share in the pains as well as the joys of the family. God became man for our sakes and shared in the sufferings of humanity, and a Christian who also shares willingly in these sufferings is thus 'honoured' and 'blessed' (Matt. 5.11, 12) to share God's life. The philosopher Descartes said, 'I think, therefore I am'. But it is more true to say 'I suffer, therefore I am'; I suffer, therefore I become what God created me to become.

2. We see suffering as an 'honour' when we can see a purpose for it. This is why Paul wrote, 'for his sake'. To suffer because we are Christians shows the world how much we value Jesus Christ.

The same conflict which you saw and now hear to be mine (v. 30): Paul's readers had seen him engaged in conflict and suffering at Philippi (Acts 16.19–40). Perhaps the jailer who made him suffer was one of these readers. Paul and his readers were engaged in the same 'conflict' in which Christians must be engaged in every generation and in every place. And Paul, like all great leaders, only urged his readers to endure what he himself had endured.

STUDY SUGGESTIONS

WORDS

1. 'Striving side by side' (v. 27b). Give 3 examples of situations in which you would use the word 'striving' to describe the activity of a Christian congregation.
2. Which four of the following words have the same or nearly the same meaning as 'omen' in v. 28?
   dream   sign   warning   chance   omission   forecast   report   hint   opinion
3. 'Grace' (v. 29). How has this word been translated into another language which you know? What is the full meaning of that word? How good a translation is it?

CONTENT

4. (a) What were the three chief causes of disunity among the congregation at Philippi?
   (b) Why was it specially important for the Philippian Christians to be united?
5. 'Striving side by side' (v. 27). Explain in your own words why Paul wanted the Philippians to 'strive'.
6. What evidence of Paul's quality as a great leader do we find in v. 30?

BIBLE

7. ' "Worthy of the gospel" does not mean that a Christian's behaviour can ever *earn* God's approval' (p. 41)
   (i) What does 'worthy of the gospel' (v. 27a) mean?
   (ii) In which four of the following verses does the word 'worthy' mean the same as in Philippians 1.27? What is its meaning in each of the other verses?
   (a) Mark 1.7   (b) Acts 5.41   (c) Acts 26.20   (d) Eph. 4.1
   (e) Colossians 1.10   (f) 1 Timothy 6.1   (g) Revelation 5.12.

DISCUSSION AND RESEARCH

8. 'Christians show their love for God . . . by the way they relate to other people' (p. 41).
    (a) How much do Christians mix with non-Christians in your town or village? On what occasions? What sort of relationship exists between Christians and others?
    (b) What differences are there, if any, between the ways in which Christians relate to their fellow Christians, and the ways in which they relate to their fellow-citizens in general?
9. How would you answer a fellow Christian who said 'A truly spiritual person is not concerned with the affairs of the world.'?
10. 'They are following past heroes instead of Jesus Christ' (p. 43). What happens to a congregation if it does this? What 'past heroes', if any, might you yourself (or your congregation) be tempted to follow, instead of Jesus?
11. 'In one spirit' (v. 27b).
    (a) To what extent are the different 'denominations' or branches of Christ's Church working toward greater unity in your country?
    (b) How important is it that all the Churches become one Church? Do you think that is God's will? Give reasons for your answer.
    (c) Has your congregation any links with congregations in other parts of the country or with Christians in another country?
12. 'Destruction' (1.28). In your Church how do most ministers interpret this word? As total annihilation or permanent separation from God, or eventual forgiveness, or something else? How do *you* interpret it?
13. (a) When you have heard about Christians who 'suffer' (v. 29) by being severely persecuted, why were they persecuted?
    (b) What effect has this persecution had on those who are persecuted?
14. (a) What would your own answer be to the question on p. 44: 'How can anyone regard it as a duty or an honour to suffer?'
    (b) Is it only Christians who regard suffering as a privilege? Give reasons and examples in support of your answers.

2.1–4

Fellowship among Christians

INTRODUCTION

In these verses Paul again appealed to the Christians at Corinth to be united (see also 1.27). He made his appeal with great gentleness, but he would not have made it at all if there had not been serious divisions in the congregation.

There were many reasons for divisions at Philippi. The Church there was composed of people of different tribes and castes, some were well-educated and some uneducated; some were rich and some poor; some were slaves, some were free; some wanted to hold on to old Jewish rituals, some wanted to be free of them (3.1–11); some felt themselves to be superior to the others (3.12–16); two of the women members were failing to work in harmony (4.2). In addition, the congregation was lively and progressive. (When there is much activity in a Church, there are often different opinions as to how it should be conducted.)

As well as urging them to be united, Paul drew attention here both to those attitudes which produce unity (see notes on 'of the same mind' in v. 2, 'humility' in v. 3, and 'look to the interests of others' in v. 4); and also to the attitudes which destroy unity (see notes on 'selfishness' and 'conceit' in v. 3 and 'look to his own interests' in v. 4).

We notice once more how personal this letter was. Paul wrote with authority, 'Be united because you cannot do your work otherwise', but he added, 'Be united so as to complete my joy' (v. 2).

NOTES AND INTERPRETATION

So if there is any encouragement in Christ (v. 1a): The word translated here 'encouragement' is used in two rather different ways in the NT:
(a) Support, comfort, consolation (e.g. in 2 Thess. 2.16);
(b) Appeal, request, exhortation (e.g. in 2 Cor. 8.17).
We find the same Greek word (*paraclete*) in John 16.7 where it refers to the Holy Spirit. It is there translated 'comforter', 'counsellor', 'helper'. Literally it means 'the one called in (like a senior doctor or a legal adviser) to be beside someone in need'.

Just as this word is interpreted in two ways, so the whole of v. 1 can be interpreted in two ways:

1. Perhaps it describes the support which the Philippians had experienced. If this is the right interpretation, then the verse means:
'Seeing that, in your life in Christ, you have received encouragement, and have been comforted by God's love, and have shared the same Spirit, and already have some affection for others and sympathy with them, *then* let this bear fruit and produce unity. So you will complete my joy . . .'

2. Perhaps it describes the appeal which Paul was making. If this is the true interpretation, then it means:
'If my exhortation given "in Christ" has any power to influence you, if my appeal which comes from love can move you, if our common participation in the Spirit is important to you, if I can appeal to you on the grounds of my affection for you and sympathy with you, *then* complete my joy by being united . . .'

Most scholars interpret the verse in the second way.

In the following story we see how a present-day apostle appealed to a congregation to be united.

There is a village in the north of Israel where the people are all Arabs and all members of the Christian ('Orthodox') Church. But in 1970 they were divided against each other so deeply that there were even brothers who would not speak to each other.

In that place Palm Sunday was the most important Church festival. On that Sunday in 1970 the children so much wanted to take part in the procession that they persuaded their parents to come to church. So all the people came together. But one group sat on one side, and the other group on the other side. Neither group looked at the other.

During the service the priest locked the doors and said to them all, 'For a long time I have tried to bring you together, but you refused. Now that you are all here and cannot escape, please either fight each other (and I will conduct the funeral of those who are killed) or be reconciled.'

For ten minutes there was silence. Then one man stood up and said, 'I forgive everyone and I ask to be forgiven by everyone.' The priest went to him and kissed him on each shoulder. Then the man walked across the church and, following the example of the priest, kissed all those on the other side of the church. Then all the people, for more than one hour, kissed one another. The service ended at 10 a.m., and from 10 a.m. till 5 p.m. the people went to each other's houses, and drank coffee with each other.

Any affection and sympathy (v. 1b): The word translated 'affection' literally means 'bowels', because people thought that their feelings were actually situated in the bowels. Both words, 'affection' and 'sympathy', mean compassion, a gift which God has given to all people and not only Christians. But Jesus Christ, by His coming into the world, made it possible for human beings to be more deeply compassionate than before. There is a letter in a museum which was written in the year 1 BC by a man to his wife who was expecting a baby. He had gone to Alexandria in search of work, and wrote: 'If you give birth to this child, let it live if it is a male. If it is a female, throw it out.'

Compare the attitude of that father with the compassion of a Christian doctor called Vedabodikam in Tirunelveli, South India. He discovered that there were a great many lepers living in a village called 'Satan's Pool' who could not get treatment from the hospital twelve miles away because the sand was too hot for their bare feet. So, with the help of friends, he built a simple treatment centre in their own district. But the elders of the village fiercely opposed him, and at the same time his own wife died, and the centre had to be closed. It was after ten years' more work, when Dr Vedabodikam was seventy-seven, that the centre was finally re-opened, with enough accommodation for thirty men and thirty women to receive in-patient treatment, both Hindus and Christians. They are, as God's children, becoming what God created them to be, through one man's compassion.

But such feelings of compassion and affection are deep-rooted in each person, and do not always come to the surface. Christians and Christian leaders need to be aware of these feelings because they are God's gifts. We need also to express them to one another. We are less useful to others if we can only use our minds and not our hearts. A group of Christians in England were accustomed to sit quietly for most of their worship and to listen in silence to long sermons. One day they were invited to worship with Pentecostalists from the Caribbean. One of them said afterwards: 'Those Pentecostalists were very emotional and noisy. When they were saying goodbye to one of their members who was going overseas they were all weeping and wailing as the leader prayed. We felt very uncomfortable, and could not understand why they behaved like that.'

Being of the same mind (v. 2): Note also the phrases 'having the same love', 'being in full accord', 'of one mind'. In all these phrases Paul was answering the question, 'What produces unity?'

1. Having unity is not the same as holding exactly the same opinions, e.g. about the interpretation of the Bible or about applying the gospel to modern politics. Members are united if they are aiming at the same goals, loving the same Lord. In an orchestra the musicians do not all play the same note, but they produce a good sound together because they have the same aim: i.e. to play the music as the composer planned it should be played. See note on 1.27.

2. When members can each contribute their own special gifts there is unity. This is clearly true when we think of the unity of the Church as a whole. A fully unified Church will be a Church where each part or

denomination contributes its own traditions and its own special understanding of God's will, and lives in the way its members believe that God intends life to be lived. It will not be a Church where everyone thinks exactly alike.

Do nothing from selfishness or conceit (v. 3a): These are the first two words Paul used to answer the question, 'What destroys unity?'

Selfishness means the desire above all for one's own personal advantage rather than for the good of the whole Church.

It means the desire of one village to gain greater praise from the Church leaders than other villages. Great bitterness resulted when one mistaken Church official told village congregations to see 'which one can contribute most to the Building Fund'.

It means the desire of a party or faction within a congregation above all to defeat other parties. In many congregations there are rival parties who oppose each other, and even go to court over such matters as property or marriages or alleged insults or appointment to leadership.

All this results in a spirit of bitter rivalry rather than co-operation.

Conceit means false or empty pride. There is a good sort of pride, when someone recognizes the gifts which God has given him and uses them and thanks God for them. And there is also a false sort of pride. A falsely-proud 'conceited' person is one who pretends that he is a better person and is more valuable because he has been given special gifts (forgetting Paul's words in 1 Corinthians 4.7: 'What have you that you did not receive?'). Such a person is more anxious to receive praise, or to be well-known or admired or listened to, than to do the work which he has been given.

In humility count others better than yourselves (v. 3b):

Humility: As in v. 2 Paul here answered the question, 'What produces unity?' A 'humble' person is one who accepts the truth about himself, and does not pretend to have developed as a Christian more than he really has. A humble person is willing to be corrected. The word here translated 'humility' did not exist before the coming of Christ. Only someone who, through Christ, can believe in God's forgiveness can dare to be humble. There are people who pretend to be worse than they are, and refuse all responsibility on the grounds that they are 'nobody'. These are *not* humble people. But the more truly-humble people there are in a congregation, the more the members are united. See Romans 12.3–5: 'I bid every one among you not to think of himself more highly than he ought . . . but according to the measure of faith which God has assigned him. For . . . we, though many, are one body in Christ, and individually members one of another.'

Count others better: The word translated 'better' does not mean better in character. Paul was not saying here that a Christian should pretend

'Being of the same mind' (2.2). 'Unity is not the same as holding the same opinions . . . it means aiming at the same goals . . . where members can each contribute their own special gifts' (p. 49).

The members of Stillman College choir in Alabama, USA, certainly seem to be 'of the same mind' though they are not all singing the same note. How far, in your congregation, are members 'aiming at the same goals' and 'each contributing their own gifts'?

that everyone else is a better Christian or a more expert teacher than he is. He meant that a truly 'humble' person sees Christ in the people whom he meets, and can say 'Praise God that you have qualities which I do not possess.' This agrees with the words of 1 Peter 5.5, 6, where it is said that a humble person is first of all humble before God and as a result humble with other people.

Look not only to his own interests, but also to the interests of others (v. 4): Christians are right to make plans and to pray for themselves, their families and their friends, and to rejoice in the gifts God has given them. But always at the same time they must plan and pray for other people and rejoice in *their* gifts. So, once again, Paul was saying, 'If you do this, you will be united'.

STUDY SUGGESTIONS

WORDS

1. 'The word here translated "encouragement" is used in two different ways in the NT' (p. 47).
   (a) Divide the following words into two lists according to whether they mean 'support' or 'appeal':
      console   cheer   urge   comfort   incite   sustain   stir up   persuade
   (b) Which meaning does the word 'encouragement' have in (i) 1 Corinthians 14.3; (ii) 1 Thessalonians 2.11?
2. Paul used the phrase 'having the same love' to describe an attitude which brings unity between people. Find 5 other phrases in the passage Philippians 1.27—2.4 which he used for the same purpose.

CONTENT

3. (a) What 2 attitudes did Paul describe as *destroying* unity in a congregation?
   (b) What 2 attitudes did he describe as *creating* unity?
4. What do we learn from v. 2 about the relationship between Paul and the Philippians?
5. In what way is the message of Philippians 2.1–4 the same as the message of 1.27–30?

BIBLE

6. 'Pride' can mean two quite different attitudes: false or empty pride on the one hand, or a good sort of pride (see p. 50). Which sort of pride: (i) false or (ii) good, is meant in each of the following passages?
   (a) Mark 7.21–23   (b) 2 Corinthians 5.11, 12   (c) 2 Corinthians 7.4   (d) 2 Corinthians 7.14, 15   (e) 1 John 2.15–17.

DISCUSSION AND RESEARCH

7. Give two examples from everyday life of people showing false pride, and two examples of people showing good pride. What was the effect on other people in each case?

8. 'Count others better than yourselves' (v. 3). In a Church discussion group one member said, 'Truly humble Christians should always count others first and themselves last.' Another said, 'But Jesus told us to love our neighbours *as* ourselves. If we always put ourselves last we are denying everyone else the position of being last.' A third said, 'I think these words encourage hypocrisy. Ordinary Christians can pretend that they are counting everyone else better than themselves, but they can't really do so.'

    What is your opinion? Which member best understood what Paul meant in v. 3?

9. What is your opinion of the action taken by the Arab priest as described on p. 48? What would you have done? Who made it possible for the reconciliation to take place?

10. 'We are less useful to others if we can only use our minds and not our hearts' (p. 49).

    Do the members of your congregation chiefly use their minds or their hearts, in their relationships with each other and with those outside the Church? In what ways, if any, could they be more 'useful to others' if they expressed their feelings of compassion more openly?

2.5–11

Jesus Christ the Servant

INTRODUCTION

In 2.1–4 Paul had urged his readers to be united. But how could this be done? Disunity and war are the natural ways in which humans live. How could unity and peace 'break out'? How could the Philippians learn to 'count others better than themselves'?

Paul answered in vv 5–11: 'Only by being open to receive the spirit of Jesus Christ, the truly humble one, the servant.'

In these verses he was continuing his teaching about the attitude of Christians towards each other. It may seem at first sight that Paul was trying to describe carefully and fully what sort of existence Jesus had before He became man, or in what way He was both God and man. But if we study the letter as a whole, and especially 1.27—2.11, we shall see that Paul's chief aim was to change the attitude of Church members to each other. He was saying 'If members have the Spirit of Jesus the Servant within them, they will look for ways of serving each other rather than looking for status and privilege.'

The thoughts are:

1. 'Let your attitude to one another be like Christ's attitude to mankind' (v. 5).

2. 'He accepted humiliation and suffering and death for their sake' (vv 6–8).

3. 'But in doing so, He was raised to His full self, He was exalted' (vv 9–11).

Note: It may be that in vv 6–11 Paul was quoting from a hymn written by someone else which was used in Church services at that time. Reasons for thinking this are:

(a) In Greek this passage has a rhythm like a hymn or song that is sung. Also it divides up into six verses each of the same length, like a hymn.

(b) It refers to the cross of Christ but (contrary to Paul's custom) does not add 'for our sakes'. Also, contrary to Paul's custom, it makes no reference to Christ's resurrection.

NOTES AND INTERPRETATION

He was in the form of God (v. 6a): The 'form of God' is the 'nature of God', so that this means 'Jesus shared God's nature'.

We cannot tell from these words whether (a) the writer meant that Jesus 'had always been God by nature' (Phillips) or (b) he was referring to Jesus's life on earth.

Most scholars believe that the first of these interpretations is correct: 'Divine nature was his from the first' (NEB). We find that Paul expressed this belief (that Jesus had existed since the beginning of creation) in other letters also: e.g. 1 Corinthians 8.6: 'Jesus Christ, through whom are all things and through whom we exist'.

Christians do not all have the same attitude to this belief. Some say: 'It must be so. If Jesus was not one with God from the beginning, then He was never God. He could not start being God at a later date. This is why Paul repeated it so often.' Others say: 'Paul had no evidence for his statements about Jesus's existing from the beginning. If Jesus shared in the creation of the world, how could He be truly human?'

As we have seen, in this passage Paul was aiming at changing the Philippians' behaviour rather than explaining these matters to them. It is as if, in writing or quoting these words, he was saying, 'Christ shared and shares God's nature, and God's nature has always been self-giving love. Meditate on this, and you will live in fellowship together.'

He did not count equality with God a thing to be grasped (v. 6b): This may mean, (a) that Jesus had no need to grasp or hold on to His equality with God because it was His by right, *or* (b) that Jesus willingly let go of His equality with God for our sakes.

The second of these interpretations seems more in keeping with the rest of vv 6–11. If we accept it, we still have two questions to ask:

1. What was meant by 'equality'? 'Equality' refers to the equal status and dignity and glory which Jesus had with God. It does not mean God's nature. Jesus never let that nature go.

2. Why did the writer use the word 'grasped'?

(a) He may have been contrasting Jesus with the rebellious angels referred to in Isaiah 14.12–14, who said, 'I will make myself like the Most High.' If so, then he thought of Jesus as refusing to 'grasp' equality in the time before He became man.

(b) But it is more likely that he contrasted Jesus with Adam, and thought of Jesus as refusing to grasp honour and privilege and status in His earthly life. Adam tried to grasp equality with God (Gen. 3.5). Christ the 'last Adam' (1 Cor. 15.45) gave away this equality.

Did the Philippians see the application of this to their own lives, as Paul hoped? Did they for the sake of others give up the desire for position and status? Christians have repeatedly failed to do so. In the past many English Christians in India believed that Hindus and Muslims would take Christ seriously if He was worshipped in magnificent buildings, and if the Church had special privileges from the Government. In fact these Christians found that such 'privileges' made their witness not easier but more difficult, because it is in humble people that most Indians expect to find God's presence.

He emptied himself, taking the form of a servant (v. 7a):

Emptied himself: These words have been translated in various ways in different Bible versions; e.g. 'stripped himself of all privilege' (Phillips); 'made himself nothing' (NEB); 'gave it all up' (GNB).

Of what did Jesus strip Himself? *Not* of His sharing of God's nature. It was God's majesty and dignity and position that He put aside when He became man. (Some think that 'emptied himself' is a quotation from Isa. 53.12 'he poured out his soul'. If this is so, then emptying refers to Christ's death, not to His becoming man.)

Many readers of this verse also ask the question: 'Did Jesus strip Himself of God's power and knowledge when He became man?' This is an important question, but it was 'status' and 'dignity' (not power or knowledge) of which Paul was thinking when he said that Jesus 'emptied himself'. However, we may note that Jesus was indeed limited in knowledge and power: 'He could do no mighty work there'

(Mark 6.5); 'Of that day . . . no one knows . . . not even the Son' (Mark 13.32). And He needed to grow as human beings do. 'Jesus increased in wisdom . . .' (Luke 2.52). If Jesus had not been limited in these ways we could not regard Him as a real human being.

To what extent did Philippian readers really follow this Jesus who was without any privileges, who shared the actual living conditions of the world by being alongside us? Paul was saying that the more they did so, the more seriously their message would be taken by the insecure and dispossessed and despairing people, by those who saw no meaning in life and believed they counted for nothing. If such people saw that the Philippians were following a Leader without privileges, then they could say, 'Jesus is one of us.'

The form of a servant: Jesus willingly became the servant of God and of the world. He did not wear the disguise of a servant, but really *was* a servant ('form' means 'real nature', as in v. 6). Jesus was not a helpless 'slave', but He did experience humiliation and was always under orders. (A servant serves in someone else's house, not his own.) The writer probably had in mind the 'Servant' of Isaiah 42.1–4, and Jesus may have been referring to Isaiah when He described Himself as having come 'not to be served but to serve' (Mark 10.45).

How can followers of Jesus also live as servants of God and of the world? It seems that we are not naturally willing to be servants. In a girls' secondary school a class was about to read a Shakespeare play. The teacher said, 'We need someone to read the part of the servant.' But no girl was willing, and the teacher had to read the part herself.

But the more an individual Christian or the Church as a whole willingly behaves as a servant, the more Christlike they become. It was Rabindranath Tagore, the great Indian Hindu philosopher who said to Christians (who at that time had great privileges in India), 'I beg you to be more like your Jesus.' Some Churches and some Church leaders have status and privilege and need to let go of them. Others have no status or privilege and need to accept their Christlike positions willingly.

Born in the likeness of men (v. 7b): The words mean that Jesus looked like a man, and everyone could see that He was a man. This repeats what was said in the first part of the verse. It does *not* mean that He was only 'like' a human being. Paul was not making the mistake of saying that Jesus was God and that He only 'appeared' to be a human being. This mistaken belief is referred to in 1 John 4.2: 'Every spirit which confesses that Jesus Christ has come in the flesh is of God'. If Jesus had not been fully man, He could not have mediated between God and man.

Being found in human form he humbled himself and became obedient unto death, even death on a cross (v. 8):

'Have this mind among yourselves, which is yours in Christ Jesus, who . . . emptied himself, taking the form of a servant' (2.5–7).

The man bandaging a patient's foot while others wait for treatment is headmaster of the local school on Ulithi, in the Caroline Islands. In his free time he gives this sort of service because there are so few doctors there, and so few other volunteers. Why do you think there are so few volunteers? Why are so few people willing to be a 'servant'?

In human form: i.e. 'fully sharing our human nature'.

He humbled himself: not only by becoming man, but in His life as man (see note on humility, in 2.3b).

Became obedient unto death: We find one account of this in Mark 14. In Gethsemane Jesus was faced with the decision, whether to escape death or to accept it, and we read of His obedience in v. 36, 'Not what I will, but what thou wilt'.

Usually in the NT writers point to the results of Jesus's death (see Romans 5.19: 'By one man's obedience many will be made righteous.') But in this verse the death of Jesus is a sign that there were no limits to His obedience to the Father and no limits to His self-giving to mankind. See John 13.1 (the beginning of John's account of the suffering and death of Jesus), 'Now he was to show the full extent of his love' (NEB).

There are many non-Christians who see the death of Jesus in this way. The Hindu Gandhi saw the self-sacrifice of Jesus on the cross as a perfect example of *satyagraha*, because Jesus was innocent and yet suffered. It is true that Gandhi saw the death of Jesus only as a supreme 'example' and could never believe that by His death Jesus 'cleanses us from all sin' (1 John 1.7). But Jesus's death always inspired and stimulated Gandhi and his followers, and indeed many non-Christian Indians still go to Christian churches on Good Friday. Buddhists regard quietness and separateness as the most important qualities in life, but many of them are attracted by Jesus who totally let go of his quietness and separateness by dying for the sake of others.

Most Muslims regard the death of Jesus as failure, and because they honour him as a prophet they say that He did not die (Koran. Sura 4.156, 157). But Muslims pay great respect to someone who gives his life for others.

Christian Churches can only witness to non-Christians if they follow the self-giving which Jesus showed by His death. As we have seen, this means individuals giving up the desire to get their own way. It may mean Churches being willing to give up privileges, and to give up their existence as separate Churches in order to achieve the greater unity of the whole Church.

Death on a cross: To be put to death would have been terrible enough, but Jesus was put to death *on a cross*:

(a) Philippians, living in a Roman colony, where crucifixion was used to kill common criminals, could see for themselves what a terrible death it was.

(b) Jews, following Deuteronomy 21.23: ('a hanged man is accursed by God'), believed that anyone killed on a cross was cursed, and therefore separated from the love of God (see Gal. 3.13). There were no limits to the self-giving of Jesus.

Therefore God had highly exalted him, and bestowed on him the name which is above every name (v. 9):
Therefore: i.e. *because* Jesus willingly gave up His position of honour and His life, He was exalted. (Compare the exaltation in Isaiah 52.13 of the 'servant' of Isaiah 42.1–4). In the NT writers do not regard this exaltation as a reward, but as a part of the willing selfgiving. According to John 13.31, when Judas had left the Last Supper in order to betray Jesus, Jesus said 'Now is the Son of man *glorified*.' See Matthew 18.4: 'Whoever humbles himself . . . *is* the greatest.' These writers were not guessing about the condition of Jesus after His life on earth. They wrote from their own experience that being humbled willingly *is* exaltation (see note on 'glory' in 4.20).

On the surface it seems nonsense to say that being brought low is being exalted. It is good sense only to those who have experienced it, to those who have 'given themselves away' (i.e. emptied themselves of status), and discovered that they had 'found themselves'. (See Matthew 10.39: 'He who loses his life for my sake will find it'.) This verse (Phil. 2.9), like the whole passage (vv 5–11), cannot be understood until it is lived.
Bestowed on him the name: The Greek word translated 'bestowed' is the same word which is translated 'granted' in 1.29. (See note on p. 44.)

What is the name which Jesus received? In the Bible 'name' means much more than the word which distinguishes one person from another, such as 'Joshua', 'Elizabeth'.

(a) It means the character or nature of the person. 'Whatever you ask in my name [i.e. according to my character], I will do it.' (John 14.13).

(b) It often means a new stage of a person's existence, especially being given the power or authority or 'rank' to do some special work. This is its meaning in this verse and in Matthew 16.18: 'you are Peter'. It was a new stage for Abraham when God made a covenant with him and gave him a new name (Gen. 17.5). It was a new stage for Jacob when he met God 'face to face' and God gave him a new name (Gen. 32.28–30).
Above every name: As Peter said (Acts 4.12): 'There is no other name under heaven . . . by which we must be saved.' Jesus is therefore unique among human beings and their religious leaders. But by saying this Christians do not mean that there is no truth at all in other religions. Peter also said, 'God shows no partiality, but in every nation anyone who fears him and does what is right is acceptable to him' (Acts 10.34, 35). God is greater than His Church, and gives His Spirit to those outside it as well as to its members.
At the name of Jesus every knee should bow (v. 10):
At the name of Jesus: The correct translation from the Greek is '*in* the name of Jesus', that is, we can approach God in worship because Jesus has made it possible for us to do so. Jesus is the way. We live and worship in His name.

Every knee: i.e. all creation, the angels, and all human beings, both the living and the departed. See also 'every tongue' in v. 11.

Note: 'Should bow' rather than 'shall bow', i.e. all creation 'ought to' accept His authority because He is *worthy* to be treated in this way.

The Church sees here one of its chief aims. It has many good aims, e.g. to defend itself in the face of opposition, to increase its membership, to stand up for those who are being unjustly treated. But it is not less important to bring people to place themselves gladly under the authority of Jesus. This task is very great indeed. Although there are many in other religions who secretly honour Jesus as 'Lord', there are many more who either despise Him or have never heard of Him. In China the number of Christians has doubled in the past thirty years, but out of 1,000 million Chinese, still only one in 200 can be called Christian. In spite of this, He is worthy of worship by everyone, and the Church exists to proclaim this.

Bow: There are Christians who interpret this to mean, 'When you hear the name "Jesus" in a Church service, bow your head or bend your knees'. Many worshippers do indeed find that such actions help them to worship, but v. 10 does not refer to them. 'Bow' means 'bow in spirit' (see Isa. 45.23).

Every tongue confess that Jesus Christ is Lord (v. 11a): The theme of verses 9 and 10 is the 'exaltation' of Jesus, and it is summed up in v. 11 in the word 'Lord'. We should first note how revolutionary this sentence is. To say that Jesus who 'took the form of a servant' and 'humbled himself' and 'became obedient unto death' should be called 'Lord' turns upside down what the world regards as greatness. The world calls people 'Lord' who aim at escaping suffering, live apart from ordinary people, and give orders to others. This sentence is as revolutionary as Jesus's own words to His disciples: 'Those who are supposed to rule over the Gentiles lord it over them . . . but it shall not be so among you' (Mark 10.42, 43).

What did this word 'Lord' mean to the Philippians?

(a) Greek-speaking Jews used it to translate 'Yahweh' (Jehovah) which was the Hebrew name for God;

(b) Romans used the word when speaking of their Emperor;

(c) Romans and Greeks used it for the heathen 'gods';

(d) But for all of them the word meant 'master' or 'owner', such as the owner of a ship or house or slave.

When Christians said that Jesus was their 'Lord', they meant that they gave to Him obedience and love which they gave to no other person whom they knew. They obeyed Jesus because God had appointed Him as the head of all things. A student who was discussing this passage said, 'In this College we obey the Principal because he has been appointed by the Governing Body. Is this an illustration of how God appointed Jesus as "Lord"?'

'Jesus Christ is Lord' was the first Christian 'creed'. Candidates for baptism had to declare that they believed this creed before they could be baptized. Later candidates had to declare much more than this and the Creeds became longer and more complicated. There are Christians today who believe that the first creed should still be used as the one creed for all Christians.

To the glory of God the Father (v. 11b): i.e. Jesus desired that glory should be given to His Father, not to Himself.

Jesus, the exalted one, was still Jesus the servant, the servant of His Father God. Paul taught that, although Jesus was not 'inferior' to the Father, He was 'subject', 'answerable', 'obedient' to Him. See 1 Corinthians 15.28: 'The Son himself will be subjected to him [God] who put all things under him'.

In this verse 11b Paul was summing up the whole passage of vv 1–11. He was saying, 'You must regard Jesus as the willing Servant. He was servant of all mankind (v. 7) and He is servant to His Father. If you follow Him closely, you will be servants to one another. In this way you will become a united congregation.'

STUDY SUGGESTIONS

WORDS

1. Which 5 of the following words have the same meaning as 'name' as it is used in v. 9?

   character   title   nature   power   authority   label
   appointment   reputation

2. (a) What word is used to translate the word 'Lord' (v. 11a) in your own language or any other language you know?

   (b) In what other context is that word generally used? (For example, in modern English 'Lord' is more often used to mean someone who has been granted a title of nobility by the State as a reward for public service, rather than a master or owner.)

   (c) What effect, if any, do you think the use of the word 'Lord' as a title for Jesus has on people's ideas about Him?

CONTENT

3. What question was Paul answering in vv 5–11?

4. 'It may be that in vv 6–11 Paul was quoting from a hymn . . .' (p. 54).

   (a) For what two reasons do some people think this?

   (b) It may be that there are parts of other hymns in Colossians 1.15–18 and 1 Timothy 3.16. Which of these passages do you think is most like Phil. 2.6–11? In what ways is it similar?

5. On p. 54 we discussed two interpretations of the statement 'He was in the form of God' (v. 6a). Which interpretation do you accept? Give your reasons.
6. Of what did Jesus 'empty' Himself (v. 7a)?

BIBLE

7. 'Jesus willingly became the servant of God and of the world' (p. 56). Read the following passages and then explain what is meant by saying that Jesus became the servant (a) of God, and (b) of the world.
    Isaiah 52.13—53.8   Matthew 12.15–18   Matthew 20.25–28.
8. (i) In what ways do the following passages link up with Philippians 2.7a?
   (ii) Which of these passages do you think most closely agrees with Philippians 2.7a? Give reasons for your answer.
       (a) John 13.14   (b) Romans 8.3   (c) Hebrews 2.14.
9. 'He humbled himself' (v. 8). Say who was being humbled, according to each of the following passages, and in what ways each was also being 'exalted'.
    (a) Luke 14.7–11   (b) Luke 18.9–14   (c) Philippians 3.8.

DISCUSSION AND RESEARCH

10. (a) What is meant by the statement: 'There were no limits to the self-giving of Jesus'? (p. 58).
    (b) What do people of other religions or of no religion, whom you know, think of the self-giving of Jesus?
11. 'Being humbled willingly *is* exaltation' (p. 59). One student said that in his experience 'being humbled willingly may be exaltation, but it can also lead to conceit.' Another student said 'For me, being humbled willingly is almost impossible. I am being humbled *un*willingly all the time.' Discuss these statements with a friend in the light of your own experience.
12. To what extent is your congregation a servant to the community? To what extent could it be?
13. When a class of school-girls were reading a Shakespeare play, no girl was willing to play the part of a servant (p. 56). Why do you think no girl was willing?
14. '. . . Jesus Christ is Lord.' 'We should note how revolutionary this sentence is' (p. 60).
    (a) Why is that sentence said to be 'revolutionary'?
    (b) How far is it true to say that Jesus Himself was a 'revolutionary'?

2.12–18
Go Forward: God is at Work!

INTRODUCTION

Paul's main thought in these verses was this: 'We have seen that Christ was the supreme Servant. You will behave as servants by faithfully continuing with the work which you have begun: work to complete your salvation' (see note on v. 12b).

In these verses Paul had in mind the story of Moses, perhaps feeling that he himself had had a similar experience. He had brought the people out of their old life into a new one, but now they were grumbling and slow to go forward. His thoughts were:

1. God is at work helping you to complete what you have begun (vv 12,13).

2. Others can see that God is at work in you:
   By your humility and contentment (v. 14);
   By your distinctiveness as Christians (v. 15a);
   By your faithfulness to the gospel (vv 15b and 16a).

3. You and I have fellowship together (vv 16b–18).

NOTES AND INTERPRETATION

Therefore, my beloved (v. 12a):
Therefore: In chapter 2 Paul first declared a great truth and then said 'Therefore . . .', showing his readers how to apply the truth to their lives. He did the same in other letters; e.g. in Romans he first declared the truth that we are saved by faith in what God has done, and not by what we do; and then he said 'Therefore . . . offer yourselves to God' (Rom. 12.1, GNB).

He was saying here that if the Philippians really believed that Jesus was the supreme Servant, then they would turn their belief into behaviour. (We do not 'believe' the great statements of the Creed until we live them.)

My beloved: In these verses Paul was calling on them to make changes in the way they lived, but he did so with gentleness – 'My beloved'. Because he loved them, they could see what he meant when he taught that God loved them. So by gentleness he led them forward. Can a pastor lead people to conversion before they have become his friends?

In my presence (v. 12b): When Paul was present with them in Philippi and leading the congregation, they obeyed him. At that time Paul did not merely send them messages, he lived among them. A pastor is someone who is among his people and visiting his people's homes, not one who only preaches from a pulpit. There are times when we need someone whom we can see to be beside us. A child who slept alone at the top of a high house was frightened one night by a violent thunderstorm. His mother shouted from below, 'Don't worry. God is with you.' The child said, 'You sleep up here with God then. I am going downstairs to be with father.'

In my absence, work out your own salvation with fear and trembling (v. 12c): In my absence: It was good that Paul had lived among the Philippians, but he could not remain in Philippi for ever. And now that he was absent, they must continue to obey God.

This was a test for them. If Paul had pointed to himself rather than to God, if it was Paul only whom they had been obeying, then when he left them they would fall away from living as Christians. But if it was God Himself whom they obeyed, then Paul's absence would not seriously affect their lives. What they did when Paul went away showed what they themselves believed.

The work of a Church leader is to help members to love and obey God Himself, as revealed in the gospel about Jesus Christ. Then when the leader, or the members themselves, must go to live somewhere else, their faith is not weakened.

There is always a danger that a Church member may give his loyalty not so much to God as to the leader of the congregation (especially if the leader is a strong personality). Or he may depend too much on a friend whom he admires, or on a group of Christian friends who have supported him, or on his family. These are all God-given supports, but they too easily take the place of God Himself. An Indian teacher to whom many went for counsel expressed this in the form of a parable: 'I point with my finger and show you the moon. But you gaze at my finger and see no moon.' This is the reason why Paul then wrote: 'Work out your own salvation.' As we see in v. 13 this does not mean 'Be independent of God' nor 'You have got to do it in your own strength'. It means, 'You must now depend on God and upon each other rather than on me.'

It was easier for the Philippians when they could let Paul take their decisions for them. In the same way it is simpler for people today to have a masterful Church leader or political dictator who takes all the decisions. But when this happens the people are prevented from becoming mature.

Work out: These words really mean 'work to complete' or 'work hard at'. See note on 1.6. There was a danger that, having once been established by Paul, some members might think that their task was

'In my absence, work out your own salvation' (2.12).

These students at a theological seminary in South Africa are discovering God's will for His world with the help of their tutor. There will come a time when they will leave college and be without the tutor's help. How can the tutor best prepare them for that time?

only to maintain what they had been given. It was as if Paul was saying, 'You are like farmers who have bought some land. Go on working till harvest time!' 'You are like a bus driver. Don't throw your passengers out half way along the journey. Take them all the way!'

Your own salvation:

1. In this verse Paul was probably thinking of the spiritual health of the whole congregation. He had referred to it earlier when he wrote about right relationships in the congregation (see notes on 2.1–4). As a congregation they must learn to do without him, and grow in dependence on God and in their work of being servants to one another and to those around them. (This is also how Paul used the word 'salvation' in 1.28.)

2. But for Paul and other NT writers the word 'salvation' usually refers to individuals rather than to a group or congregation.

It means:

(a) Being rescued from ill-health or physical danger or from death. See Mark 3.4: 'Is it lawful on the sabbath to do good or to do harm, to save life or to kill?'

(b) Having 'wholeness', i.e. health of body and soul (see Luke 17.19 'thy faith hath made thee whole', AV). New Testament writers thought of a person as a whole person. They did not (as many people, including some Christians, do today) regard a human being as a collection of separate parts – 'body', 'mind', 'spirit'. See note on 'Body' in 3.21.

(c) Being rescued by God through Jesus Christ from the overwhelming power of our sins (Matt. 1.21) and from being for ever separated from God. See Mark 8.35: 'For whoever would save his life will lose it, and whoever loses his life for my sake and the gospel's will save it.'

When does salvation take place? On the one hand writers say that a person 'has been saved' (Eph. 2.8). This means that this person has gratefully accepted God's offer of salvation. On the other hand, this person still has a long way to go and so he is still 'being saved' (Acts 2.47), and his salvation needs to be completed in the future (Romans 5.9: 'We shall be saved by him from the wrath of God').

With fear and trembling: Paul was not referring to the sort of fear that prevents a person from taking action, as a rabbit is paralysed by its fear of an approaching fox or a lizard by its fear of a snake. Nor, of course, did Paul want his readers to doubt the love and mercy of God. 'With fear and trembling' means honestly facing our weaknesses as a congregation, and as individuals, knowing our own special temptations, never taking for granted that the way we do things is the way that God wants them done. It means depending on God's grace, as Paul showed in v. 13 (see also 2 Cor. 7.15).

For God is at work in you, both to will and to work for his good pleasure (v. 13): That is, 'You do not have to do this in your own strength alone.

God's spirit is at work in you. He creates in you the desire ('will') to do what He wants done, and the power ('work') to do it.'

1. At first sight there seems to be a contradiction between 'working' (v. 12) and letting God work (v. 13). But when Christians put these two verses into practice, there is no contradiction. We become our best selves when we most fully let God control us, just as a sailor in a small sailing boat catches the wind. He controls the boat, so as to make the most of the wind. But he cannot provide the power that drives the boat along.

A mother and father who care for their son are 'at work in him', so to speak, giving him their love, setting him an example, and inspiring him with a goal in life. Yet at the same time they want him to take decisions for himself and to become the unique individual that God intends him to become.

Any leader of a study group has to work hard to help each member to take a proper share of the study and discussion. He is 'working' (v. 12). But he can at the same time be aware that God's Holy Spirit is there, to come into the group, making it possible for the members to trust each other, or to understand an important truth in a way that at first seemed impossible.

2. No one who really believes that God 'is at work' in them can boast of their own achievements. See 1 Corinthians 4.7: 'What have you that you did not receive?' A boastful Christian is as ridiculous as a student who won the first prize for an essay, but who (it was discovered later) had copied the whole essay out of a book.

3. It is part of the 'good news' of Jesus's teaching that God is at work in us. He is at work in the minds of students as they study, in the hands of builders as they build, in the wills of those who worship Him. At the beginning of the Orthodox Church 'Liturgy' (the Holy Communion Service), the Deacon turns to the Presiding Priest and says, 'Now is the time for the Lord to take action.' Not all religions offer their members such teaching. For example there is nothing like it in the teaching of Buddhists.

Do all things without grumbling or questioning (v. 14): This is the first of the three signs by which, Paul hoped, the Philippians would show that God was at work in them. They would be humble and contented rather than grumbling or questioning. A person 'grumbles' when he feels 'I deserve something better than this'. Perhaps Paul was thinking of the grumbling of the Israelites against Moses (Exod. 16). But the Israelites' murmurings were against Moses and against God; it seems from Philippians 2.1–4 that the Philippians murmured against each other.

'Questioning' here means bitter argument or 'wrangling' in which each speaker is trying to overcome the others rather than to discover the truth.This sort of 'argument' is quite different from asking questions in order to learn from others, or to find out if we have correctly understood them. We read in Luke 2.46 that Jesus was 'asking them questions'.

In the Greek the emphasis is on the words 'all things' i.e. amongst your work-mates, your family, your fellow Church-members, your friends, at worship, at meals, in recreation.

Blameless and innocent . . . without blemish (v. 15a): The second sign which, Paul hoped, would show that God was at work in the Philippian Christians was chiefly this: that in their behaviour they would be distinguishable from those who were not Christians. The words 'blameless' and 'innocent' and 'without blemish' do not mean 'perfect' or 'without sin'. They mean 'not being a serious stumbling-block to those who are not members of the Church', 'not making it impossible for other people to believe in Jesus Christ'. See note on 1.10.

Innocent: This means sincere, having good motives.

Without blemish: This is a phrase which Jewish worshippers used to describe an offering which was fit to be sacrificed (see v.17 and the references to sacrifice). We could translate it 'fit to be God's servant'.

Children of God . . . in the midst of a crooked and perverse generation amongst whom you shine as lights in the world (v. 15b):

Children of God: It is clear that Paul had in mind Deuteronomy 32.5 when he wrote this. But according to Deuteronomy the Israelites had ceased to behave like God's children, and it was they who were 'crooked and perverse'. According to v. 15b, on the other hand, the Philippians were still God's children in spite of their failures.

In the midst: They were in the midst of the world. Jesus prayed that His disciples would be *in* the world, but not *of* the world, i.e. Christians should be in communication with the people around them, but should not depend on those people for leadership and inspiration (see John 17.15, 16: 'I do not pray that thou shouldst take them out of the world, but that thou shouldst keep them from the evil one.'). All members of small Christian congregations know how difficult it is to take a full part in the life of the surrounding community if most members of that community belong to other religions or practise no religion at all. But it is not more difficult for them than it was for that small Christian congregation in the great Greek city of Philippi.

God has placed His Church 'in the midst' of His world. Its members are not being faithful to Him if they spend so much time on Church affairs that they are ignorant of the events taking place elsewhere. When in 2 Corinthians 6.17 Paul wrote 'come out from them and be separate' (thinking of Isaiah 52.11) he meant 'Be distinctively Christian. Be different in the way you live'. He was not telling them to retreat from the world into an enclosed society of Christians. There is a church in a Swiss town which has one wall made entirely of glass. The pastor said, 'As we worship we are aware of the people outside whom God will send us out to serve.' During the Second World War the German Dictator Hitler met the Christian leader Martin Niemoller and ordered him to limit his activities to Church events. He said to Niemoller, 'I will take care of the German people.' Niemoller replied, 'But we too, as Christians, have a responsibility towards the German people. That responsibility was entrusted to us by God Himself. Neither you nor anyone else in the world has the power to take it from us.'

It is important that Christians look carefully at the world in which they live, in order to see in what ways it is 'crooked' and 'perverse'. In a group which did this, one member said 'It is crooked because it thinks that the *biggest* things are the best things.' Another said, 'Because it has no hope. It believes that unity among nations is impossible.'

So Christian students in a college or Christian nurses in a hospital or Christian workers in a big office are to take full part in the activities of the college or hospital or office. If the only meetings they attend are Christian meetings, they are forgetting Jesus's words as recorded in John 17.

The 'world': The Greek word is *'cosmos'* and has the following meanings in the New Testament:

(a) The whole universe which God has created (Matt. 25.34).

(b) Those who fail to acknowledge God's authority: 'The world hates me' (John 7.7). This is the meaning in v. 15b.

(c) Those whom God is for ever working to win back from disobedience to obedience (see 2 Cor. 5.19: 'God was in Christ reconciling the world to himself').

The 'generation' of that time and the 'world' in which they lived were 'ungodly', 'crooked' and 'perverse', like a table which can only be used with difficulty because the legs have become warped and crooked. As a result they were blind to the truth about Christ, and therefore persecuted the Church (see 1.28–30).

You shine as lights in the world ('stars in a dark world' NEB): i.e. 'You are different from the world. If you quarrel with each other in the congregation, or divide up into separate parties, you can no longer be points of light.' 'Let your light so shine . . .' (Matt. 5.16). But Paul did not mean that the Philippian Christians were 'superior' to other Philippians. As a spectator said about one of the teams while watching a football match, 'These players are not better than the other players, but they have a better captain.'

Holding fast the word of life (v. 16a): This is the third sign that God was at work in the Philippians.

Holding fast: i.e. keeping something safe which God had entrusted to them; holding it firmly, like a servant guarding the house carefully while the owner is away. (Another interpretation is that it means 'holding it out for all to see, offering it to everyone'.)

How do Christians 'hold the gospel fast'? Not by storing it away, like the servant in Jesus's parable who hid his talent (Matt. 25.25), but by using it, studying it, opening themselves to it so that it affects the way they live.

The word: In the Bible, writers use the word 'word' in several ways: e.g.:

(a) God's will (Gen. 1.3: 'God *said*, "let there be light";').

(b) God's will which He communicates to mankind through His messengers (Isa. 38.4: 'the word of the Lord came to Isaiah').

(c) God's will as it has been written down in the first five books of the Bible (Psalm 119. 42: 'I trust in thy word').

(d) Jesus Christ Himself who perfectly expressed God's will (John 1.1: 'the Word was with God').

(e) The 'good news' or 'gospel' which Christians preach (Acts 13.44: 'They gathered to hear the word of God'). This is its meaning in this verse. It does not mean the Bible or the New Testament. They did not exist as such when Paul wrote.

The word of life: This means 'the good news through which the life of God Himself has come into you, and by which you now live'.

So that in the day of Christ I may be proud that I did not run ... or labour in vain (v. 16b). Some readers are surprised or troubled to see that Paul drew attention to himself in vv 16–18, as he did in 2.2. They believe that a Church leader should hide his own feelings from those whom he leads. But one of the reasons why Paul was able to lead congregations was that he treated them as his friends, with whom he could openly and honestly share his joys and his hopes and his fears and his doubts. See also 2 Corinthians 6.11: 'Our mouth is open to you', i.e. 'We have spoken very frankly to you' (NEB).

Paul wrote v. 16 with a feeling which most Church leaders have sometimes felt: 'What will all my work lead to in the end? Is it really worth while?' Paul gave his own reply: 'I am praying that you, as a congregation, will complete your salvation (v. 12), live in humility (v. 14), be distinctive as Christians (v. 15), and hold firmly to the gospel (v. 16a), so that in the end I shall know that my work was worth while.'

He used the words 'run' and 'labour' because he, like his readers, knew about the Greek Games. He had probably watched them. There were many different sorts of athletics, but the chief sort was running. The training for these races was very strenuous indeed. As Paul used the word 'labour', the readers could picture the sweat pouring off the runner as he went around the course time after time under a burning sun. See note on 3.14.

As the runners hope that they will receive a reward, so Paul prayed that he would in the end have a reward, and be 'proud' that he had achieved his object. For 'in the day of Christ' see note on 1.6b. For 'pride' or 'glory' see note on 3.3.

If I am to be poured as a libation (v. 17): In v. 16 readers could picture the games. As they read v. 17 they pictured a priest pouring a 'libation' (which he did during the games), i.e. spilling wine on to the ground as part of a sacrifice, usually the last part. This was a common thing to see in those days, just as it is a common custom among many tribes and peoples today. In several countries wine is poured out when a new ship is launched or a new house is completed.

Paul clothed his thoughts in words and picture-language which were familiar to his readers.

In writing this verse he had four special thoughts:

1. He might very soon be executed: 'even if I am to be poured . . .' (This is a different thought from those in 1.24 and 2.24).

2. If so, his death would be like a sacrifice: 'poured as a libation'.

3. His death would be in fellowship with the sacrifice which the Philippians were already making: 'upon (i.e. following on) the sacrificial offering of your faith'. Their faith expressed itself in many sorts of service (see 4.14), and so Paul calls it a sacrifice. (He used the Greek word which is usually translated as 'liturgy', which means a priestly ministry).

4. He rejoiced and wanted them to rejoice too. The Philippians could rejoice both at the sacrifice which they themselves made and at Paul's death if it should take place soon.

It may seem astonishing that Paul could write in this way. But vv 17 and 18 are only a summing-up of what he was saying throughout the whole letter: to accept suffering ('to be poured as a libation') and to be in fellowship with them ('poured upon the offering of your faith') – this is joy ('rejoice with me'). Christians of many nations, and at different times, have shown the same willingness to 'be poured out'. In 1977 Archbishop Luwum of Uganda became convinced that he and the other bishops there must make a strong protest to Idi Amin who was then President of Uganda. The President's soldiers had been allowed to destroy churches and kill Christians and very many others in an attempt to suppress opposition. But to protest was to risk death. As Jenani Luwum set out with the letter of protest he said, 'Even if he kills me, my blood will save the nation.' When he was arrested, he whispered to a brother-bishop, 'They are going to kill me. I am not afraid.' He was shot on 16 February 1977, without a trial.

Oscar Romero was a shy man who became Archbishop of El Salvador. At first he supported the Government and had no sympathy for Christian priests who opposed it. But as he watched Government soldiers killing very poor people rather than feeding them, he changed his mind. He said to soldiers, 'When you hear the words of a man telling you to kill, remember instead the words of God, "Thou shalt not kill". God's law must prevail.' Friends tried to persuade him to be silent. He said, 'As a shepherd I am obliged by divine law to give my life for those I love.' He was shot through the heart at 6.30 pm on 24 March 1980, as he was saying the words of the Mass in a small hospital chapel: 'This is my body which is given for you.'

STUDY SUGGESTIONS

WORDS

1. (a) What 3 meanings does the Greek word here translated 'world' have in the NT?
   (b) Which of these meanings does it have in v. 15?
2. (a) What sort of 'fear' was Paul talking about in v. 12?
   (b) Which 5 of the following words do *not* mean the sort of fear he meant in that verse?
   worry humility submission terror panic awe respect concern mistrust obedience alarm
3. What is the full meaning of the phrase 'word of life' in v. 16?

CONTENT

4. Why did Paul begin v. 12 with the word 'Therefore'?
5. In what way was Paul's absence a 'test' for the Philippians?
6. (a) What were the three 'signs' which would show that God was 'at work' in the Philippians?
   (b) What sort of behaviour might prevent them from 'shining as lights in the world'?
7. 'So that . . . I may be proud' (v. 16b). See note on 2.3a. Which sort of pride was Paul talking about here?
8. Which two phrases in this passage refer to traditional ritual practices of Paul's time?

BIBLE

9. Which verses or phrases in 2.12–18 contain the same or nearly the same thought or teaching as that in each of the following?
   (a) John 17.15, 16 (b) Matthew 5.16 (c) Acts 13.47
   (d) Philippians 4.4 (e) 2 Timothy 4.6.

DISCUSSION AND RESEARCH

10. 'Without grumbling' (v. 14). What do you most often grumble about? How is it that some people hardly ever grumble?
11. 'Work out your own salvation' does *not* mean 'Be independent of God' (p. 64). What does it mean?

12. 'If the leader is a strong personality' (p. 64). What difficulties are likely to arise in a congregation where the ordained leader is very masterful, so that members depend on him to take all the decisions?

13. '*When* does salvation take place? (p. 66). Some Christians take such verses as Ephesians 2.5 and 5.8 to mean that they are fully 'saved' as soon as they accept God's grace and commit their lives to Christ. Others believe that although God continually offers His grace, each person's salvation remains to be completed in the future. What is the teaching of your Church on this subject? What are some specially good effects of this teaching? What, if any, are the bad effects?

14. 'A feeling which most Church leaders have sometimes felt: "What will all my work lead to in the end? Is it really worth while?"' (p. 70). Some Christians think that leaders should hide such feelings. What was Paul's attitude? What is your own opinion?

15. 'Poured as a libation', i.e. like a sacrifice. 'Paul clothed his thoughts in words and picture-language which were familiar to his readers.' (p. 71). What sort of picture-language would you use today to express the idea of 'sacrifice' if you were speaking:
    (a) to a village congregation in a mainly Muslim area of West Africa?
    (b) in a seamen's mission in a busy port in South-east Asia?
    (c) in a large industrial city of Europe or America?
    (d) to your own congregation (unless included above)?

2.19–30
Fellow Workers

INTRODUCTION

We discover in these verses the special reason why Paul wrote this letter: because he was so anxious (v. 20) about the lack of unity among the Philippians. He had decided that as he could not go himself he must send Timothy and Epaphroditus to them, as his representatives. But since the Philippians might not welcome them, he had to prepare them for the visit. So he wrote this letter.

Most of this passage (vv 19–30) concerns Paul's own position as their leader and his relationship with his fellow workers. Vv 19–24 concern Paul and Timothy, vv 25–30 Paul and Epaphroditus.

We note here how Paul was able to work with people younger than himself (v. 22), and how he suffered alongside them (vv 27, 28).

We can also see what sort of relationship Paul had with those with whom he worked from phrases such as the following: 'fellow worker' (v. 25), 'father' and 'son' (v. 22), 'brother, and 'fellow soldier' (v. 25), 'yokefellow' (4.3), 'fellow servant' (Col. 1.7 and 4.7), 'fellow prisoner' (Col. 4.10).

It is likely that by nature Paul did not find it easy to work with other people (see note on 1.15). But in spite of this, and because of the help of God, he did work with them effectively.

NOTES AND INTERPRETATION

I hope in the Lord Jesus to send Timothy (v. 19a):
Hope in the Lord: i.e. 'I plan, if the Lord is willing'. See also v. 24: 'Trust in the Lord that . . .'. Paul believed that it was right to make plans, but that he should not put too much confidence in them. He might soon be killed. So he put himself humbly into God's hands, believing that God would be honoured, whether he himself lived or died (see 1.20).
To send Timothy: Paul planned to send Timothy to Philippi, but not until it was clear what was going to happen to himself in prison.

Paul had first met Timothy in Lystra (Acts 16.1), and had him circumcised so that Jews as well as Gentiles would accept him. After that Timothy was with Paul on many of his journeys, as we see from Acts 17—19; and he was with Paul in prison (1.1).

We may note especially:

(a) Timothy's *faithfulness*. He genuinely cared about the well-being of the Philippians (v. 20). He sincerely wanted to give honour to Christ (v. 21). People had discovered these qualities over a long period – 'you know his worth' (v. 22a). This is the reason why Paul planned to send him.

(b) His *willingness to take second place*. Messengers and junior typists are not treated as important people in most communities. But Timothy was happy to be Paul's messenger (1 Cor. 4.17; 16.10; 1 Thess. 3.6); and to help Paul with many of his letters (2 Cor. 1.1; 1 Thess. 1.1; 2 Thess 1.1; as well as Phil. 1.1). Those who take the lead and those who take second place are equally 'important' in the Church.

(c) His *overcoming of disadvantages*. We see from 1 Timothy 4.12 that some people were unwilling to listen to Timothy because he was young. Also it may be that, because he was the child of a mixed marriage (Greek and Jew), neither Greeks nor Jews fully accepted him, although he had the advantage of inheriting the best traditions of both races. Whatever disadvantages there were, he overcame them.

(d) His *willingness to suffer* for the gospel. Like Paul he was imprisoned (see Heb. 13.23).

So that I may be cheered (v. 19b):

1. Paul so much wanted the Philippi congregation to be united that he was unhappy until he could receive news that this had taken place. He refused to take disunity for granted (see also v. 28: 'that I may be less anxious').

Unity would come more quickly to congregations and to the whole of God's Church if more members were unhappy about disunity.

2. Like all leaders, Paul had his own needs. This was true of Jesus, e.g. in Gethsemane (Mark 14.32–33: 'He said to his disciples, "Sit here while I pray." And he ... began to be greatly distressed and troubled'). Paul needed reassurance and fellowship. But did his readers understand this? How far do congregations today understand the needs of their leaders and support them with their prayers?

3. In the Greek this sentence is: 'so that *I also* may be cheered' – i.e. 'I as well as you'. Paul meant that both he and the Philippians themselves would be happier if the congregation was more united.

Be genuinely anxious for your welfare (v. 20): Paul felt that no one except Timothy would be really interested in the well-being of the Philippians.

The Greek word translated 'anxious' has two different meanings. (This is also true of the English phrases 'be anxious' and 'care'):

(a) In this verse it means loving someone so much that we do all we can for them. We mind very much what happens to them. Paul said that Timothy would do this. See also 1 Corinthians 12.25: 'that the members may have the same care for one another'.

(b) But in all other New Testament passages it means worrying and being afraid because we do not trust God enough (see Matt. 6.25: 'do not be anxious about your life, what you shall eat').

They all look after their own interests, not those of Jesus Christ (v. 21): At first sight it seems that Paul was angrily condemning the whole local congregation, and that he was surely exaggerating. But 'all' probably means 'all the Christians in this place whom I have so far approached'.

What Paul meant was: 'The only way to encourage the Philippians to live in fellowship is to send a messenger. Letters of advice are not enough. But that messenger needs to be someone who loves Jesus Christ and loves the Christians more than he loves his own advancement.'

As a son with a father he has served with me in the gospel (v. 22): A fuller translation of the Greek would be: 'As a son to a father, he served as a slave along with me in the work of preaching the Gospel.'

Son with a father: This describes the relationship between Timothy and Paul (see pp 73, 74).

Served: We have seen (pp 4 and 5) some of the ways in which Paul and Timothy served Jesus Christ like slaves. They were His willing slaves, just as Jesus Himself was a 'slave' or 'servant' (2.7).

To send to you Epaphroditus (v. 25a): The Philippians had sent Epaphroditus to Paul with a present of money (see 4.18), and so that he could look after Paul in prison. While Epaphroditus was there he became very ill (v. 27). The Philippians heard about his illness and were distressed. Then Epaphroditus heard about their distress and, having recovered from his illness, wanted to return to Philippi and to show them that he was well again (v. 26). And Paul encouraged him to go.

Probably he did this for two reasons: first, because Epaphroditus wanted to go: secondly, because Paul thought that Epaphroditus was the right sort of person to work for unity in the congregation (v. 28).

The name 'Epaphroditus' is interesting because it contains the name of the pagan Greek goddess 'Aphrodite'. It seems that when Greeks became Christian, they did not think it necessary to throw away a name which they had used before being baptized. Does this offer any guidance to those, for example, whose names contain the word 'Allah' (the Muslim word for God) e.g. Abdullah, and who are later baptized?

My brother and fellow worker and fellow soldier (v. 25b): These are words which, as we have seen, describe the relationship between Paul and one of his junior colleagues.

brother: see note on 1.12.

fellow worker: see pp 73, 74.

fellow soldier: one who shares suffering and danger. The words point to the way in which a Christian shares a relationship, shares work, and shares a common fight.

Your messenger and minister to my need (v. 25c):

1. Epaphroditus was a *messenger*. The Greek word is *apostolos*, which means someone who is 'sent'.

(a) Usually in the New Testament it means one of the Twelve Apostles whom Jesus sent to be His representatives (Mark 6.30).

(b) There were others later who were called 'apostles', along with the Twelve, e.g. Paul and Barnabas (Acts 14.14).

(c) In two places (here and 2 Cor. 8.23) it refers to other people who were sent to represent a congregation officially. It was in this way that Epaphroditus was an 'apostle'.

2. He was a *minister*. The Greek word is *leitourgos*, which meant someone who offered service to God.

In Greek cities it meant someone who served the public by making a generous gift to a city, e.g. by paying for the training of their athletes, and who was therefore very much honoured. Paul used the word here to show that Epaphroditus, by making his visit, was both making an offering to God by worshipping Him (see Acts 13.2) and also serving the public (see 2 Cor. 9.12).

God had mercy on him (v. 27): Paul meant that God had enabled Epaphroditus to recover from his illness.

To many readers today this seems a strange way of saying that he was cured of his illness. But it is strange only if we forget that when a patient is healed there are many causes of the healing. The first cause is God's own Spirit, but there are different sorts of 'secondary' causes which God inspires: the patient's own bodily powers, the care and prayers of his family and friends, the doctor and the medicines he uses. Paul and other writers in the Bible draw attention chiefly to the first cause, God Himself. So Paul wrote here, 'God had mercy'. Most people today consider only the secondary causes, and forget that these are inspired by God. Christians need to take seriously all causes of healing.

The word 'mercy' in the Bible means:

(a) God's tender compassion, His pity for the weakness and sadness of mankind (e.g. Luke 1.50: 'His mercy is on those who fear him from generation to generation').

(b) The compassion that God calls on people to show to one another (e.g. Luke 10.36, 37: ' . . . "which of these proved neighbour to the man?" He said, "The one who showed mercy on him." And Jesus said to him, "Go and do likewise." ').

Receive him in the Lord with all joy (v. 29a): The way in which a Christian congregation 'receives' people is important, whether they are its own members (as Epaphroditus was) or strangers. Paul said 'in the Lord' (i.e. as the Lord receives all who come to Him), and 'with all joy'.

'Receiving' is much more than giving a word of welcome: it is caring for visitors, showing them that they are now among friends and no longer strangers, getting to know them and introducing them to other members and looking after them.

Honour such men, for he nearly died for the work of Christ (vv 29b and 30): That is, 'honour Epaphroditus because he worked for Christ and in doing so nearly died.' It was his desire to work for Christ and the work which he did, for which they should honour him, not his serious illness. There have been Christians who have become ill through ignorance or self-neglect. There have been others who have been martyred because they were mentally sick. It is the *motive*, and the love with which Christians serve Christ, that we honour, not their unhappiness or illness or failure or death.

Risking his life to complete your service to me (v. 30b): that is, risking his life by giving service which you, being far away, could not give.

The word translated here as 'risking' is a word used by gamblers. Epaphroditus had 'gambled with his life' by being the friend of Paul who might soon be executed.

In the 3rd century AD there was a society of Christians called 'The Gamblers'. They risked their lives in looking after insane or dangerous people, or those who had the plague or other infectious diseases. Such love and courage is wonderful and unusual. But all Christians have to take some risks in order to achieve any change in the Church or in the world. They risk making mistakes, being misunderstood, falling into temptations that are too great for them. 'If you don't take risks, you'll never take anything'. said a famous soldier. 'Taking risks in the service of Christ' is one way of describing 'faith in Christ'.

STUDY SUGGESTIONS

WORDS

1. 'Genuinely anxious for your welfare' (p. 75). The word 'anxious' has two chief meanings.
   (a) Which one of the following words has the same or nearly the same meaning as 'anxious' in v. 28?
   serious   grave   frightened   caring   worried
   interested in   suspicious
   (b) Does the word 'anxious' in v. 28 have the same meaning as in v. 20? If not, which two of the above words are closest in meaning to 'anxious' as used in v. 20?

CONTENT

2. '"Receiving" is much more than giving a word of welcome' (p. 77) or merely accepting a gift. What 'more' than this does 'receiving' mean in v. 29?
3. What do we learn from this passage about the special reason why Paul wrote to the Philippians?
4. What four qualities did Timothy have that specially fitted him to be God's messenger to the Philippians?
5. What do we learn from this passage about Paul's relationship with his fellow workers?
6. 'God had mercy' (v. 27). To whom did God show mercy according to Paul in this verse? What did God's mercy do for them?
7. Why had the Philippians sent Epaphroditus to Paul, and what had happened to him as a result?

BIBLE

8. 'Your messenger' (v. 25c). This translates the Greek word 'apostolos' which occurs in the following passages. Say in each case whether the word refers to: (i) the Twelve, (ii) others called 'apostles', or (iii) people sent with a message.
   (a) Luke 24.10   (b) John 13.16   (c) Rom. 1.1
   (d) 1 Cor. 15.7   (e) 1 Cor. 15.9   (f) 2 Cor. 8.23
   (g) Phil. 2.25

9. In what way did people experience the 'mercy' of God or man in each of the following passages?
(a) Deut. 7.9 (b) Luke 1.50–55 (c) Luke 10.33–37
(d) Luke 18.35–42 (e) 1 Pet. 1.3

DISCUSSION AND RESEARCH

10. In Paul's description of Timothy (v. 19a) we note four qualities that made him a good helper and messenger. What *other* qualities, if any, do you think can help to make a person a good helper and messenger or representative?
11. 'How far do congregations today understand the needs of their leaders and support them with their prayers?' (p. 75). What is your answer to this question? Give examples.
12. 'They all look after their own interests' (v. 21). Congregations today are often accused of looking after their own interests. Do you think this accusation is a true one? If so, what are the reasons, and how can such groups of Christians be encouraged to be less selfish?
13. Fellow-soldiers (2.25).
(a) In what way should a Christian be a 'fighter'?
(b) What are the dangers of thinking of the Church as an 'army' and Christians as 'soldiers'?
14. 'God had mercy' (2.27). How do most Christians expect to be healed when they are ill – (a) by God directly after prayer by the patient? (b) by God directly after prayer by a group? (c) by traditional doctors and medicine? (d) by modern doctors and medicine? (e) by other means?
15. Epaphroditus nearly died for the work of Christ – but 'all Christians have to take some risks' (p. 78). What risks, if any, have you yourself ever taken on account of being a Christian? How would you answer someone who said, 'Risking one's life can never be right. It is just another way of committing suicide.'?

3.1–11

The Old Way and the New

INTRODUCTION

In the first two chapters Paul wrote mainly about the need for the Philippian Christians to be united. In this chapter 3 he changed the subject. The subject is now a comparison between:
1. The 'old' way in which Paul had previously approached God and in which (in his experience) many Jews still did approach God; and

'In chapter 3 . . .' there is 'a comparison between the "old" way in which Paul had previously approached God, and the "new" way' (pp 79–81).

A Taiwanese mechanic guides Swaziland farmers, who had used old farming methods all their lives, to use new methods of ploughing. What 'old ways' of approaching God are Christians today most tempted to adopt? Whose task is it to guide them towards the 'new' ways?

2. The 'new' way in which Paul now approached Him.

Paul compared these two ways much more fully in his letters to the Galatians (see Gal. 3.1–4) and Romans (see Rom. 8.1–8). In Philippians 3.2–11 the chief differences he was referring to are:

The 'old' way: Paul had once believed, and some Jews still believed, that they could be accepted by God through their own good deeds, and by being circumcised. He referred to all this as 'confidence in the flesh' (vv 3 and 4).

The 'new' way: Christians believe (Paul said) that God accepts them because of what Jesus did and in spite of their sinfulness ('glory in Christ Jesus', v. 3).

The passage can be summarized as follows: (v. 1 stands on its own and is not connected with vv 2–11):

A *warning* against a group who were trying to bring the Christians in Philippi back to the old way (vv. 2, 3).

Paul's own *past experience* – of the failure of the 'old way' to bring him righteousness (vv 4–7).

Paul's *aim for the future* – that he might grow in the righteousness which he had found through Christ (vv 8–11).

Note: Some Christians who read these verses fall into one of two errors – they *either* regard them as an attack on the Jewish religion, *or* they feel satisfied that they are not like those whom Paul criticized. We shall avoid these errors if we remember that:

(a) Paul was referring to his own past experience and (probably) to a group of Jews in Philippi. He was not attacking the Jewish religion as such.

(b) All religious people (and certainly all Christians) are tempted to fall into the mistaken way of living which Paul here called having 'confidence in the flesh', or justifying themselves before God and their fellow-humans. See note on v. 3b.

NOTES AND INTERPRETATION

Finally, my brethren, rejoice in the Lord (v. 1a):

Finally: Why did Paul write 'finally' but not bring his letter to an end? Scholars have made various suggestions, as follows:

(a) Some have suggested that Paul, having written 'Finally', remembered that he had something else that he wanted to say. We all do this in writing letters, especially if we are dictating to a secretary as Paul was. In this case he wanted to add a warning to his readers. So without crossing out 'Finally', he gave his warning, beginning at v. 2. It seems that he also did this in his first letter to the Thessalonians (see 1 Thess. 4.1).

(b) Others think that Paul was just about to end his letter when a messenger arrived from Philippi with news about false teaching which the Christians were receiving, and that he immediately attacked this false teaching.

(c) Others believe that vv 2–19 are part of a different letter which Paul wrote at another time. They think that, when Paul's letters were being collected together, editors mistakenly included these verses with this chapter.

Readers may ask, 'Does it matter how vv 2–19 were written?' The answer is that in interpreting any part of the Bible, we are more likely to discover the ideas which the writer wanted to express if we know who the writer was, and when and in what circumstances he was writing it. If we do not do this, we are in danger of thinking the passage means what we ourselves *want* it to mean. But in the case of vv 2–19, whichever suggestion we accept, it was clearly Paul himself who wrote these verses.

Rejoice in the Lord: Paul wrote about rejoicing in 1.18 and 2.18. But here and in 4.4 he wrote 'Rejoice *in the Lord*', meaning 'Be glad with the gladness that comes from depending on the Lord Himself rather than on changing circumstances' (see note on 4.4). Some translations have 'Farewell' instead of 'Rejoice'. The Greek word can have either meaning.

To write the same things to you is not irksome (3.1b):
The same things: What were these 'things' about which, it seems, Paul had already written to the Philippians? Paul may have been referring to his teaching, (a) about rejoicing, or (b) about unity (as in chapters 1 and 2), or (c) about the false teaching which he later described in vv 2–11. We cannot tell.

Whatever teaching Paul was thinking of, he had probably given it to the Philippians in one of the letters which he wrote but which we do not have. Paul was travelling round the Eastern Mediterranean, visiting congregations and writing to them, for about sixteen years, but we have only a few of his letters. He may have written hundreds more letters which have since been lost.

If this is so, it means that we possess only a small part of Paul's teaching. In the letters which are lost he probably gave fuller teaching on matters which concern us today, such as the person of Jesus and problems of Christian conduct.

Not irksome: i.e. 'I never get tired of saying this'. Teachers and preachers need to repeat what they have said. We can all enjoy and benefit from hearing a good story over and over again. The more often we hear an idea repeated (though not necessarily in the same words), the better we remember it. A well-known preacher who was asked how he constructed his sermons said: 'First I tell them what I'm going to tell them, then I tell them, and then I tell them what I've told them.' And the great truths about God and mankind that need to be taught, year after year, never become 'irksome'. Part of the value of having Church festivals, such as Christmas, Easter, and Pentecost, is that stories are repeated. These are the stories on which Christians base their faith. In the same way, an important part of the Holy Communion service is that the leader repeats the story of the Last Supper each time. See the phrase, 'safe for you' (v. 1b), i.e. 'you can rely on these things'.

Look out for the dogs (v. 2a):

Look out: i.e. Watch out for them because they are dangerous. Christians should try to be friends with everyone, but they need to watch out for false teaching which could weaken the Church. They need to be 'watchmen' (Ezek. 3.17).

The dogs: When Paul wrote 'dogs' he was probably referring to non-Christian Jews who were persecuting the congregation in Philippi and trying to persuade the members to join (or return to) the Jewish faith. (Some people believe that by 'dogs' Paul meant Christians who taught that it was necessary for followers of Christ to keep the old Jewish laws.)

Why did Paul use such violent and discourteous language, comparing these people to the half-wild mongrel dogs who lived on garbage outside the city? His words are surprising because he usually spoke about the Jews respectfully (see Rom. 10.1; 11.1, 2). He probably wrote so strongly because he was very worried that the Christians in Philippi might be won over to the teaching of these 'dogs'. When people are worried they often become angry. Paul, being a human being, may have been angry for the same reason. As he said in v. 12, he was far from being perfect. Like all humans he had both goodness and badness. (Unlike most humans he knew how to get his badness forgiven.)

Look out for the evil workers, look out for those who mutilate the flesh (v. 2b): Evil workers and 'those who mutilate' are two more phrases with which Paul refers to that Jewish group in Philippi. 'Mutilate the flesh' is Paul's angry way of referring to circumcision. He did not criticize them merely because they were circumcised or wanted to be, but he did attack those who said that God would not accept people unless they were circumcised.

We are the true circumcision, who worship God in spirit (v. 3a):

True circumcision: According to Gen. 17.9–11 Jews were circumcised as a sign of the covenant between God and Abraham. It distinguished Jews from other races, just as today in many parts of the world the circumcision of males (and often females) distinguishes one tribe from another.

Paul used the word 'mutilate' in v. 2 rather than the proper word for Jewish circumcision, because he wanted to teach that it was the

Christians (not the Jews) who were practising true circumcision. Old Testament prophets had long ago shown what real circumcision is: e.g.: 'the Lord will circumcise your *heart* and the heart of your descendants, so that you will love Him with all your heart and soul . . .' (Deut. 30.6). But later many Jews forgot that teaching. According to Romans 2.29, 'real circumcision is a matter of the heart, spiritual and not literal', i.e. facing our own sinfulness, letting God forgive it, and sincerely intending to cut it out. (To what extent does circumcision among those who practise it today symbolize spiritual dedication?)

This was a very important verse for the Philippians to read. It explained clearly that it was *not* necessary to be physically circumcised in order to be accepted by God. The Jews, as we know, taught that circumcision *was* necessary. This was the main difference between the 'new way' Paul had taught the Philippians to follow, and the 'old way' of those Jews who did not accept his teaching.

Worship God in Spirit: This is how Paul referred to true circumcision, i.e. spiritual circumcision rather than physical. In some manuscripts the phrase is 'worship *by* the Spirit of God'.

The Greek word translated 'spirit' is '*pneuma*', and it has many meanings in the New Testament, e.g.:

(a) Wind or breath (see Luke 8.54, 55; 'He called, "Child, arise". And her spirit returned').

(b) A person's 'self', his heart, his soul, his thinking, his feeling (see Luke 1.47: 'My soul magnifies the Lord, and my spirit rejoices in God my Saviour').

(c) An invisible force for good or evil (for 'evil spirit' see Acts 5.16: 'those afflicted with unclean spirits').

(d) The spirit of God, or the Holy Spirit, i.e. the very life of God Himself flowing into the lives of human beings (as in Phil. 2.1 and in this verse).

Glory in Christ Jesus, and put no confidence in the flesh (v. 3b): There is a contrast in this sentence:

(a) Some of the Christians were proud of what Christ Jesus had done, and relied on Him because it was through Him that they were acceptable to God. This is 'glorying in Christ'.

(b) Others relied chiefly on their own outward performances, and their efforts to keep the religious rules, and did not admit that they depended totally on God's grace. This is 'putting confidence in the flesh'. See note on 'flesh' in 1.22.

Although Paul was contrasting a Jewish way of behaving with a truly Christian way, what he said applies also to mankind as a whole. A letter appeared recently in a Lahore (Pakistan) newspaper, of which the editor is a Muslim: 'I am eighteen years old. I have committed sins, and have tasted of nearly every forbidden fruit of the tree of life. Can you tell me how I can avoid going to hell? I have been to see a mullah and he has told me to repent. But that is no help, for I do not know how to repent. I have enjoyed too much doing the things that I have done.' In reply the Editor said, in the next issue of the newspaper, 'There is only one way to wipe out your bad deeds, and that is by good deeds.'

Paul's teaching applies also to Christians. All Christians are tempted at some time or another to 'put confidence in the flesh'. When they give in to this temptation, their way of life shows that they believe that they will be more acceptable to God if they perform enough good deeds, pay their Church subscriptions, attend Church services regularly, marry one wife only, or say their prayers every day. Paul's teaching was that these are good and necessary things to do, but that God accepts people and enters into fellowship with them because of Jesus Christ, not because of their good deeds.

Glory: The word translated 'glory' can also mean 'boast'. Paul used the word in two different ways: (1) To trust in oneself or in one's race rather than in God; to be 'puffed up' about one's own achievements (see 1 Cor. 4.7: 'If then you received it, why do you boast as if it were not a gift?'). (2) To celebrate with joy the achievements of Christ. This is its meaning here. (In 2 Cor. 11.30 Paul wrote that he boasted of his weaknesses because it was when he was weak that the power of Christ was most clearly seen.)

This word is quite different from the Greek word which is also translated 'glory' in 4.20 (see note on that verse).

If any other man thinks he has reason for confidence in the flesh, I have more (v. 4): that is, 'It is not because I have failed to fulfil the Jewish laws and ceremonies that I am criticizing them. I have not become a Christian just because I was an unsuccessful Jew.' Paul meant that he was not like the fox in Aesop's fable who could not reach the grapes and so said that they were sour. Then in vv 5 and 6 he said that he had kept the Jewish law more strictly than most Jews. He made a list of six ways in which he was a strict Jew:

1. '*Circumcised on the eighth day*' (v. 5a): I come from a family who kept the law strictly (see Lev. 12.3).

2. '*Of the people of Israel*' (v. 5b): I was a Jew by birth. I was not one of those Gentile 'proselytes', who had been welcomed into the Jewish community from outside.

3. '*Of the tribe of Benjamin*' (v. 5c): I belong to the tribe which gave the Jewish nation its first king, Saul. (This reminds us of what the people said to John the Baptist; 'We have Abraham as our father', Matt. 3.9.)

4. '*A Hebrew born of Hebrews*' (v. 5d): Both my parents were

Hebrews who trained me in the use of the Hebrew language, even though we lived in a Greek city.

5. *'As to the law a Pharisee'* (v. 5e): A member of the sect whom everyone respected because they kept both the written law and the traditions more strictly than anyone. Jesus criticized the Pharisees for their self-satisfaction in their achievements, not for their strictness (see Matt. 23.27: 'You are like whitewashed tombs which outwardly appear beautiful').

6. *'A persecutor of the church'* (v. 6a); I was so keen to be a faithful Jew that I used violence to attack the followers of Jesus.

From the verses that follow (vv 6–11) it is clear that Paul made this list only in order to show that nothing that he himself did could make him accepted and forgiven by God. Something different, something more, was needed (Matt. 5.20).

As to righteousness under the law blameless (v. 6b): In these words Paul summed up his list of ways in which he had kept the Jewish law. Two words are especially important:

Righteousness:

1. The Greek word here translated 'righteousness' was used in the lawcourts and means 'being judged innocent'. It is sometimes translated 'justification'.

2. But in the Bible as a whole, the word refers to the sort of behaviour which is in accordance with God's will and which brings human beings into a right relationship with God (see Deut. 6.25: 'it will be righteousness for us if we are careful to do all this commandment before the Lord our God, as he has commanded us').

3. Amongst many Jews it came to mean being innocent or being in a right relationship with God because of keeping the law. Paul called this 'righteousness under the law'. He said that merely keeping the law in this way had not brought him true righteousness.

4. But Paul had found another sort of righteousness, that is the true 'righteousness which is through faith in Christ' (see note on v. 9).

Law:

1. The word first meant God's law or God's will (see 2 Kings 17.13: 'the Lord warned Israel and Judah . . . "Keep my commandments in accordance with all the law . . . which I sent to you by the prophets"').

2. Then it was used for the first five books of the Old Testament, i.e. the Pentateuch. The word 'Law' was also used for the interpretation of the Pentateuch which was handed down among the Jews by word of mouth.

3. Later it sometimes meant the whole of the Old Testament, as in Matthew 5.18: 'not a dot will pass from the law', or the rules for conduct which we find in the Old Testament, as in Romans 13.8, 9.

4. In this verse (and in many other passages) Paul used the word 'law' to mean a false way of treating God's laws, i.e. thinking that we can keep them through our own strength and so earn God's approval (see Rom. 8.3: 'God has done what the law could not do').

When we live according to law in this false way, bad results follow. For example:

(a) We regard a visible deed as more important than our motive for doing it or a root change of heart (Matt. 6.16).

(b) We give more attention to little deeds of charity than to a total self-giving (Matt. 23.23).

(c) When we are proud of keeping the rules, then we despise those who do not keep them, or who cannot because of their work (Luke 18.9 and see v. 3 of this chapter).

(d) We may claim that we have complete understanding and authority instead of admitting to the imperfection of our faith (see v. 6 and vv 12–14).

(e) Keeping the rules becomes more important to us than entering into a right relationship with God and our fellow-men (Matt. 9.13).

(f) We tend to ask 'How *little* can I do in order to keep the law?' rather than 'How *much* could I do?' (Matt. 18.21).

(g) When we find that we cannot keep the law, we despair (Rom. 7.24).

Whatever gain I had, I counted as loss for the sake of Christ (v. 7): In these verses (7 and 8) Paul compared what he had 'lost' with what he had 'gained' or could gain in the future. We are reminded of Jesus's words 'Whoever loses his life for my sake . . . will save it' (Mark 8.35), and His parable of the merchant 'who, on finding one pearl of great value, went and sold all that he had and bought it' (Matt. 13.45, 46).

Paul wrote these verses with great joy and gratitude. What he had 'gained' was of such 'surpassing worth' (v. 8).

The language Paul used is treasurer's language, it is 'profit-and-loss' language, which could be set out like this:

Loss	Profit
v. 7: 'whatever gain I had'	'Christ'
v. 8a: 'everything'	'knowing Christ Jesus'
v. 8b: 'all things'	'gain Christ and be found in Him'

But Paul only saw things in this way after his conversion. Before his conversion he put the privileges (which he had because he was a strict Jew) on the side of 'profit'. Afterwards, he felt that they were 'loss', because they encouraged him to rely on his own efforts. In this way they actually prevented him from relying on Christ, through whom he had found a right relationship with God.

I count everything as loss because of the surpassing worth of knowing Christ Jesus my Lord (v. 8a):

Loss: Paul never ceased to be a Jew, but he was glad to have given up his 'old' way of living, i.e. trying to gain God's approval by keeping the law. He was like a man who has been working all night with an oil lamp, then the dawn breaks and the lamp is no longer needed. The sun has risen.

Knowing Christ: This is an unusual phrase. Most writers refer to 'knowing God', e.g. Galatians 4.9: 'now that you have come to know God . . . how can you turn back?'

In our ordinary conversation we use the word 'knowing' in various ways. A man may 'know about' the Prime Minister of his country. Another man, who once met the Prime Minister, may say he 'knows' him. A third person, who lives and works with the Prime Minister means much more when he says he 'knows' him. In the Bible 'knowing' has an even deeper and fuller meaning. To know God, to know Christ, means to put oneself at His service, to love Him, to be loyal to Him, to commit oneself to Him. This is how Paul used the word in this verse.

My Lord: Paul was personally committed to Jesus Christ, as Thomas was when he said 'My Lord and my God!' (John 20.28). This personal religion is certainly different from a religion in which the members worship God only because they belong to a group which does so (see also Gal. 2.20: 'it is no longer I who live, but Christ who lives in me').

I have suffered the loss of all things, and count them as refuse (v. 8b): Paul was chiefly thinking here of the loss of his position and status as a strict Jew. It may be that he also had in mind the loss of his property, since he may well have been disowned by most of his family when he became a Christian.

He called his old position as a strict Jew 'refuse' or 'garbage' because it was useless. Paul felt that although the Jewish law was excellent in itself (he said so in Rom. 7.7, 12), it did not do what the Jews expected it to do. It had not, for example, brought Paul into a right relationship with God; that relationship only began through Jesus. So he turned away from 'the old way'. In this Paul was like a bald man who bought an expensive bottle of 'hair-restorer'. When he had used it for many months and no new hairs had appeared, he threw it away.

We must note that by calling his life as a Jew 'refuse' Paul was being as discourteous to the Jews as when he called his opponents 'dogs' in v. 2. It is not surprising that they were so angry in return that many of them failed to understand what he was saying. They thought that he was attacking *all* religious rules and regulations.

That I may gain Christ and be found in him (vv 8c, 9a): The two phrases 'gain Christ' and 'be found in him' mean nearly the same thing. Paul had this great hope or aim that, at every moment in his life and whatever happened to him, he would be 'in Christ' and would be seen ('be found') to be part of Christ (see note on 'in Christ' in 4.10).

Although Paul was referring here to his individual and personal relationship with Christ, he made it plain in other writings that neither he nor any other Christian could have this relationship in isolation from other Christians. He told the congregation at Corinth that it was the 'body of Christ', and that each member was a limb belonging to that body. The limb could not exist on its own (1 Cor. 12.27). Similarly Jesus said that He was the Vine and His followers were the branches. No branch could bear fruit unless it continued to grow 'in' Him (John 15.1–8). When someone has really 'gained Christ' and is 'found in Him', he does not continue as a believer unless he lives and works in fellowship with the other branches of the vine, with the other limbs of the body.

Not having a righteousness of my own, based on law, but that which is through faith in Christ, the righteousness from God (v. 9b): Paul again made a comparison:

1. He had tried to reach 'righteousness' (or a right relationship with God) through his own efforts ('of my own'), and to be a record-breaker in keeping the law strictly ('based on law'). But as we have already seen, that way had failed.

2. Now he had found a different way to righteousness. He described this way by two phrases:

(a) 'Through faith in Christ', i.e. righteousness was given to him not as a reward for his own efforts, but because he trusted that Christ had made it possible by His living and dying and rising again (see Rom. 1.16, 17: 'The gospel . . . is the power of God for salvation to every one who has faith . . . in it the righteousness of God is revealed').

(b) 'From God', i.e. righteousness was God's free gift of forgiveness, given to him although he did not deserve it (see Rom. 3.21–24: 'since all have sinned . . . they are justified by his grace as a gift').

Abdul Masih was the first Muslim in India who became an ordained Christian minister. When he was converted, five senior

Muslims made a long journey to persuade him to change his mind. In the following conversation between them we are further helped to see the meaning of this verse:

Abdul Masih: God bless you for having taken such trouble for a poor sinner like me, who has no refuge but Christ.

One of the Muslims: God has not such a shameless creature anywhere on earth.

Abdul Masih: That is true. I am even worse than you describe.

Another Muslim: How will you answer this before God?

Abdul Masih: Indeed, I do not know what I can answer. But I hope in the word that the Lord Jesus Christ has Himself spoken: 'I came, not to call the righteous but sinners to repentance.' I firmly trust that He and no one else will answer for me . . .

After further conversation, one of the visitors said, 'May God give you understanding', to which Abdul Masih said, 'Amen'.

Through this verse and other verses like it (e.g. Eph. 2.8 and 9: 'by grace you have been saved through faith; and this is . . . the gift of God – not because of works') a great many human beings in every generation have taken the step of 'faith' which Paul took and have begun the Christian journey.

Faith: Note that the same Greek word which is translated 'to have faith in' is also translated 'to believe in', 'to have confidence in', 'to rely on', 'to trust', 'to be loyal to'.

1. In the Bible 'having faith' means having faith in God's faithfulness, trusting in God's trustworthiness. So in using the word we chiefly have in mind God's nature rather than our own attitude (Isa. 26.4: 'the Lord God is an everlasting rock').

2. In the Gospels those who 'had faith' had faith in God as He was at work in Jesus. Jesus said that having faith was the opposite of being afraid (see Mark 5.36: 'Do not fear, only believe').

3. In John's Gospel the word had an extra meaning. Those who 'had faith' not only relied on God, but followed the One whom He had sent as the final truth. The word almost means 'obey Jesus' in John's Gospel (see John 14.12: 'He who has faith in me will do what I am doing', NEB).

4. As we have seen, Paul emphasized that the faithfulness of God (on which we rely) is offered to us as a gift. We cannot earn it (Eph. 2.8). Everyone, however sinful, is offered it, and 'having faith' is the act of accepting it. (Thus 'having faith' never means sitting down and doing nothing.)

5. In the letter to the Hebrews 'having faith' is almost the same as 'having hope', because it is relying on God's faithfulness as regards the future (see Heb. 11.1: 'Faith is the assurance of things hoped for').

6. If a Christian has faith in God he can 'let go and let God', i.e. he is willing to take a risk because God is reliable. But New Testament writers never contrast 'having faith' with 'knowing'. They never suggested that 'having faith' means 'believing blindly' or merely guessing. For them 'having faith in God' went *alongside* the knowledge which they had, because of their experience of His presence in their lives, and because of the evidence which they had received of His love and forgiveness.

7. After the New Testament had been written, some Christians used the word 'faith' in a new way, i.e. 'the teaching which the Church gives'. It almost has that meaning in 1 Timothy 4.1–6: 'a good minister . . . nourished on the words of the faith'.

That I may know him and the power of his resurrection (v. 10a): In the previous verses Paul had showed his readers the way in which he became a Christian. In verses 10 and 11 he explained in four phrases what he was now aiming at. 'That I may know' refers to his aim and goal.

This, the first of the phrases, means 'I want to get to the stage where I not only know Christ (see note on v. 8a), but can be more open to His power, the power of Christ who is risen and alive'. Although Paul said that this was his goal, he had of course already begun to learn how to accept this 'power'. It had raised him out of the temptations of the world, and out of physical exhaustion as he made his journeys.

Power:

1. Writers in the Bible had two great truths in mind when they wrote about 'power': first that human beings are by nature not strong enough to live without God; secondly that God possesses power and offers it to people.

2. Thus it is God's power of which we chiefly read in the Bible. Writers referred to His power because of the things which God had done in the world, e.g. Psalm 150.2: 'Praise him for his mighty deeds'.

Note that this was a very different way of thinking about God from the old Greek ideas, and from the ideas of religions such as Hinduism. The Greeks believed that a 'High God' existed but that He would have lost dignity if He had concerned himself with the activities of human beings. (There are people in the world today who model themselves on such a god!) Hindus do not call God 'creator' of the world because in their view He is so completely removed from the world that He could never become involved in it.

3. A special action of God showing His power in the world was the raising of Jesus from the dead (see Acts 2.24, 32).

4. But a result of God's raising of Jesus was that His power became

available for mankind. This is what Paul meant by 'the power of his resurrection' in v. 10. So Paul could preach effectively to the Gentiles because of that power (see Rom. 15.18, 19).

5. There are three Greek words which New Testament writers chiefly use for 'power':

(a) *'Dunamis'*, from which we get the English words 'dynamic' and 'dynamo'. In Philippians 4.13 it means God's power flowing into Paul.

(b) *'Energein'*, from which the word 'energy' comes. But *'energein'* did not mean a person's liveliness; it meant 'God at work in a person' (see Phil.2.13; 3.21b).

(c) *'Cratos'*, from which we get the word 'democrat' (people's power) (see Acts 19.20: 'The word of the Lord showed its power, spreading more and more . . .', NEB).

May share his sufferings (v. 10b): Paul's second aim was to be in such close union with Christ that he could see his own undeserved sufferings as part of Christ's sufferings. It is as if he were saying, 'Christ could not do His work for mankind without suffering. Nor can I (or His other followers) work for Him and "in Him" without suffering. But I am not just imitating what Christ did long ago; I am letting His life flow into my life' (see also Col. 1.24 and 2 Cor. 4.10).

We have already seen (p. 88) that when Paul wrote this letter he had to endure great disappointment, opposition, loneliness, anxiety (see 2 Cor. 12.10). But he was able to understand and accept his sufferings, at least partly, when he saw them as part of the sufferings of Christ.

Paul's sufferings were not unique or extreme. They were not, for example, as terrible as the sufferings of those many who are being tortured today because of their beliefs. But they *represent* all human suffering that is endured for the sake of Christ, and therefore we can learn from them.

How do human beings behave when suffering comes to them? Some are angry and puzzled and complain to God; some look for someone else to blame; some begin to notice other people's sufferings and try to lessen them; some discover other ways in which God can use them now that they are suffering. Others, like Paul, find that they can suffer in the company of Christ.

Becoming like him in his death (v. 10c): Some people think that in this sentence Paul was referring to his own physical death (which indeed may have taken place soon after he wrote this letter), and that he was saying that, when he died, he would be following in Christ's footsteps.

But it seems more probable that he was referring to dying 'to sin' as we read in Romans 6.2–11: 'How can we who died to sin still live in it?'

The difference between that passage in Romans and the phrase we are studying is that in Philippians 3.10c Paul was talking of a goal towards which he was moving, or of a change in himself that he wanted to see, not as an event that had once happened. In this verse he was saying: 'May I increasingly and every day reject (die to) all that is un-Christ-like in me.'

Perhaps Paul was here intentionally using the language of the Mystery Religions which flourished all over the Greek-speaking world at that time. In some of these religions candidates shared in a ritual in which a god symbolically died and rose again. They believed that their own natures would thus be transformed, as they united themselves with the god by means of their ritual. The great difference between this 'transformation' and the change that Paul was referring to was that in the Mystery Religions people believed that transformation took place 'magically', i.e. as the result of the right words being said and the right actions performed. Paul's 'dying to sin' was an inner surrender of himself to the will of God (see Rom. 12.2: 'Let your minds be remade and your whole nature thus transformed', NEB).

That if possible I may attain the resurrection from the dead (v. 11): Paul knew that he already had a new life, life 'in Christ' (see p. 126). In this verse he wrote about his fourth goal or hope, that after his physical death he would be given a fuller form of life in Christ.

There are many passages in Paul's letters where he expressed his belief in life after death, e.g. 2 Corinthians 5.1: 'we know that if the earthly tent we live in is destroyed, we have a building from God . . . eternal in the heavens'; Romans 8.38, 39: 'I am sure that neither death, nor life . . . nor anything else in all creation, will be able to separate us from the love of God. . . .' See also Philippians 1.22, 23; 1 Corinthians 15.12.

We may ask why Paul in this verse wrote with such hesitation: 'if possible'. Did he have doubts about life after death? The answer is two-fold. First there were times for Paul, as for all Christians, when it was easier to be confident, and times when it was less easy. No one, however deeply committed to Christ, lives permanently in the clear daylight of certainty. Secondly, in these verses (and still more in vv 12–16) Paul was pointing out with humility how much more he still needed to learn, and that he had no 'claim' on life after death. In everything he depended on God's grace.

STUDY SUGGESTIONS

WORDS

1. Paul used the word 'righteousness' three times in this passage, once in v. 6 and twice in v. 9. What were the two sorts of 'righteousness' which Paul compared in this passage?
2. What did Paul mean by 'knowing' Christ (vv 8 and 10)?
3. The Greek word translated 'Spirit' has many meanings in the NT. Which of the following meanings does it have in v. 3?
   wind   the inmost self   an invisible force   breath   a demon   the Holy Spirit of God   courage
4. (a) What does the word 'faith' usually mean when people use it in ordinary conversation?
   (b) How does its ordinary meaning differ from the Bible meaning?

CONTENT

5. We may wonder why Paul wrote 'Finally' in v. 1, but did not end his letter there. How important is it that we should know the answer to this question?
6. Two mistaken ways of understanding this passage are described on p. 81. What should we do in order to avoid these mistaken ideas?
7. (a) Who was it that Paul was telling the Philippians to 'look out for' in v. 2?
   (b) Why was he so discourteous as to call them 'dogs'?
8. What two attitudes was Paul contrasting when he said, 'Glory in Christ Jesus', and 'put no confidence in the flesh'?
9. (a) In vv 5, 6 Paul listed six ways in which he was a strict Jew. What were they?
   (b) Why did Paul count as 'refuse', or rubbish, all that he gained from being a strict Jew?
10. In what ways did Paul expect to share Christ's sufferings and become 'like him in his death' (v. 10)?

BIBLE

11. (i) 'The true circumcision' (v. 3). Which sort of circumcision did the writers refer to in each of the following verses, physical or spiritual?
   (a) Jer. 4.4   (b) Luke 1.59   (c) Acts 7.51
   (d) Acts 15.5   (e) Col. 2.11, 12

(ii) What steps do Christians take today, or what events are arranged, so that they may practise 'true' circumcision?

12. 'Faith in Christ' (v. 9b). How did people show that they had faith, according to each of the following passages?
(a) Mark 2.3–5   (b) Mark 10.46–52   (c) Luke 7.2–9
(d) Gal. 2.14–16   (e) Heb. 11.8

DISCUSSION AND RESEARCH

13. How would you answer the question on p. 84: 'To what extent does circumcision among those who practise it today symbolize spiritual dedication?'

14. 'Paul was contrasting a Jewish way of behaving with a truly Christian way . . .' but 'all Christians are tempted to "put confidence in the flesh", i.e. to live according to "law"' (p. 85).
(a) Give some examples of ways in which people in your country, both Christians and those of other religions, are tempted to live according to 'law', and describe what happens when they do.
(b) Why is it that people are so often tempted to live according to 'law', rather than depend on God's grace?

15. Think about some ways in which you yourself are tempted to live 'according to law', and then make a 'profit-and-loss table' like that on p. 87, to show what would be the 'gain' or the 'loss' for you of trying to follow Christ instead.

16. (a) No one can work for Christ or live 'in Christ' without suffering (see p. 92). What is your opinion?
(b) 'How do human beings behave when suffering comes to them?' (p. 92). In what other ways do people behave, apart from the ways outlined in that paragraph?

17. 'That I may attain the resurrection from the dead' (v. 11). Did Paul mean that he hoped to 'rise again' and be seen on earth after his death, like Jesus after His crucifixion? If not, what did he mean?

3.12–16
Christians and their Goal

INTRODUCTION

Paul wrote these verses for two reasons:

1. He wanted to prevent his readers from misunderstanding verses 2–11, where he had said that through Christ he had found righteousness. A reader might think that Paul was satisfied with his own life as a Christian. So in vv 12–16 he said, 'No! I am still a long way from being the sort of person that God means me to be.'

2. Paul wrote these verses to correct those who were too easily satisfied with their own lives. His thoughts were: 'God, in Christ, invited me to enter for a race and to win a prize. I have accepted His invitation and I am running towards the goal. But I have not yet reached it.'

NOTES AND INTERPRETATION

Not that I have already obtained this or am already perfect (v. 12a): 'This' refers to the state of completeness which Paul wrote about in vv 8–11, using such phrases as 'gain Christ' (v. 8), 'be found in' Christ (v. 9), 'having a righteousness from God' (v. 9), 'know Christ' (v. 10), 'know the power of his resurrection' (v. 10), 'share his sufferings' (v. 10), 'becoming like him in His death' (v. 10). 'All this' (v. 12 NEB) was 'the prize'.

Perfect: The Greek word which is here translated 'perfect' is translated 'mature' in v. 15. It does *not* mean 'absolutely good'.

1. Members of the Mystery Religions, which were popular in Philippi and other Greek towns, used this word. When one of them had taken part in all the ritual purifications and sacrifices, that member was called 'perfect', i.e. he had reached the highest grade. It did not mean that he was without sin.

2. For other Greek writers it usually meant 'suited to the work you are doing at present'. So a workman using an axe to cut down a tree could call his axe 'perfect' even if its handle was scratched and dirty.

3. For most of the New Testament writers it had several other meanings:

(a) The sort of person that a Christian can become at the end of this world. 'When the perfect comes' (1 Cor. 13.10). Probably this is its meaning in v. 12.

(b) Sharing to some extent (though not completely) in God's absolute goodness (See Matt. 5.48).

(c) An adult, anyone who is no longer an infant. Also a baptized member of the Church, one who is no longer a probationer, a baptized member who is developing as a disciple of Christ (see 1 Cor. 2.6 'Among the mature we do impart wisdom'). Such people do *not* think that they have reached their goal. They are more aware than other people of their own incompleteness and ignorance and sinfulness. They are growing in their awareness of Christ's will and of other people's needs (Eph. 4.13–15). They are becoming able to 'distinguish good from evil' (Heb. 5.14). They 'hunger and thirst for righteousness' (Matt. 5.6).

I press on to make it my own, because Christ Jesus has made me his own (v. 12b): i.e. 'I press forward in order to take hold of the prize, because Jesus once took hold of me.'

Press on: Paul was like a runner in a long-distance race, who kept on running towards the finishing post, even though there was still a long way to go. See note on v. 14 about Paul's use of the language of athletics.

Made me his own: What Paul was doing was the result of what Christ had done. Christ took the first step. Paul had in mind the time when he was on the road from Jerusalem to Damascus and Christ made him 'his own' or 'took hold' of him (NEB) or 'possessed' him (GNB). Because of this experience of being 'taken hold of', it is not surprising that Paul always taught that 'we are saved by grace', not by our own efforts (Eph. 2.5). See also 1 John 4.19: we love God 'because he first loved us'.

Note that there is a different translation of this verse in the NEB: 'I press on, hoping to take hold of that for which Christ once took hold of me'.

One thing I do (v. 13b): This is like a modern athlete saying, 'I have to decide whether I shall train for the 1,000 metres race or the long jump. If I try to do both, I shall not win either. I have to do "one thing".' For Paul the 'one thing' was 'running toward the goal', in the words of v. 14. He had described the goal in vv 8–11, and he saw it clearly.

Christians need to have a clear goal. For example every minister needs to ask himself from time to time, 'What am I aiming at above everything else?'

We should not interpret the words to mean that we should choose one duty and neglect other duties, e.g. that we should take prayer seriously but neglect the needs of our bodies. Nor do they mean that we should work for the conversion of others but fail to grow in our own Christian discipleship; nor that we should be concerned about our fellow members of the Church but un-concerned about other people.

'I press on toward the goal for the prize' (3.14).

Olympic competitors 'press on' in the 110 metres hurdles.

What other phrases in 3.12–14 refer to this same 'pressing on'? To what goal are you yourself as a Christian 'pressing on'?

Forgetting what lies behind and straining forward to what lies ahead (v. 13c): Forgetting what lies behind: Paul clearly did not mean that he ceased to remember his past life as a strict Jew (he remembered it well in vv 4–7). Nor did he forget his early years as a Christian (he remembered them in v. 12 and in passages such as 1 Cor. 15.3–10). He meant that it was even more important to fix his mind on the goal ahead than to look back and remember what God had done for him in the past.

Like Paul, Christians today cannot forget their past lives. But, as far as their past sins and failures are concerned, they can accept God's forgiveness instead of continually accusing themselves. As far as past success is concerned, they can thank God instead of boasting of past achievements. (There is a West African proverb: 'No one shouts "Make way!" for a man who rode a horse in days gone by.')

In the same way, although it is important for a congregation to study the past history of the Church, it is even more important for its members to be open to God's Spirit, so that they can learn from Him what to do at this present time, and what preparations they should be making for the years ahead.

Straining forward to what lies ahead: Again Paul used the language of athletics (see note on v. 14). In the early stages of a long race some runners may be somewhat relaxed, but in the later stages they 'strain forward'.

All Christians have to think out their attitude to 'what lies behind' and 'what lies ahead'. (1) There are Christians who have begun well and given their lives to Christ, but have no goal lying ahead. They are much more interested in what God once did for them than the ways in which God now wants them to grow and develop. (2) Others are enthusiastically pursuing a goal, but they find it very difficult because they have never made a break with the past and begun a new life. (3) Others are like Paul and have made a break with the past, but are chiefly interested in 'what lies ahead', i.e. what God wants them to become. See 2 Peter 3.18: '*Grow* in the grace and knowledge of our Lord', and 1 Thessalonians 4.10; 'You do love . . . but do so *more and more*' (see also Phil. 1.9).

I press on toward the goal for the prize of the upward call of God in Christ Jesus (v. 14): This is one of the many verses in which Paul compared living as a Christian to taking part in the Greek Games or athletics. There were the Olympic Games, the Games at Ephesus, and the Games at Corinth. In all of them the competitors performed many different sorts of sports, such as boxing (1 Cor. 9.26), chariot-racing, and running.

Here Paul used the language of the Games, which was familiar to his readers, in order to explain his teaching. No teachers or preachers can do their work effectively unless they understand the things which their hearers do. A minister born and educated in London went to work in a country town where many people kept pigs. 'I watched the pig-farmers at work for many months before I could usefully preach the gospel to them,' he said.

In vv 12–14 there are five phrases from which we see that Paul understood the Greek Games. He used these phrases to teach that a Christian needs to be self-disciplined and keen above everything else to reach his goal. The phrases are:

1. '*I press on*' (vv 12 and 14).
2. '*forgetting what lies behind*' (v. 13). In a track event it is important not to look back to see who is behind.
3. '*straining forward to what lies ahead*' (v. 13) i.e. not slowing down until the end is reached. How many runners have lost a race by stopping a yard from the end!
4. '*toward the goal*' (v. 14). There was a pillar at the end of the course.
5. '*for the prize*' (v. 14). The prize was a crown made from the leaves of wild olive or laurel or green parsley. Runners could see it on the finishing post as they ran towards it.

The prize: For Christians the 'prize' is complete fellowship with Christ Himself. As Paul said in v. 8 'that I may gain Christ'. The difference between Christians aiming at this prize and Greek runners aiming at their prize is that all Christians can share the prize. One Christian getting the prize will not prevent others from getting it. In the Greek games 'only one receives the prize' (1 Cor. 9.24).

Thus Paul repeated the teaching of Jesus that there is a reward for Christians. It is worth being a Christian! We remember Jesus's parable of the pearl-merchant who found one pearl of great value and who sold everything he had and bought that pearl (Matt. 13.44, 45). Paul said that Christians are like runners who give up their leisure time and their comfort in order to get the prize. They give up much in order to gain much more.

People often misunderstand this teaching and say that it is 'better' to live a Christian life because you love Christ than because you hope for a reward. But, as Paul said, there is a reward, and the reward is Christ Himself. The reward is thus an 'imperishable' crown (one that never fades, see 1 Cor. 9.25); it is not success or popularity or financial gain or comfort or status or a big family in this world.

Upward call (NEB: 'God's call to the life above').

Call: This is one of the most important words in the Bible:

1. It always means that God's loving actions come first. The good that human beings are able to do comes afterwards.
2. God's call is a call to repentance (see Luke 5.32: 'I have not come to call the righteous, but sinners to repentance'), to obedience (see

John 1.43: 'Follow me'), and to 'wholeness' (i.e. 'salvation' as in this v. 14).

3. God calls all human beings (see 1 Tim. 2.4: 'God . . . desires all men to be saved'). It is not true that He has chosen some people to have eternal life and others to lose it.

4. We hear God's call in many different ways, e.g. through other people (Luke 14.17), in a dream (Matt. 1.20).

5. We need to answer His call (see Heb. 3.7, 8: 'When you hear his voice, do not harden your hearts').

6. He calls some people, but not all, to positions of authority, e.g. in the Church (see 2 Tim. 1.6–9: 'Rekindle the gift of God that is within you . . . for God . . . called us with a holy calling').

Upward call means that God, who is 'above', calls us to share His own life. We know that 'God is Spirit' (John 4.24), and therefore is not situated in any one place, so that He is not really 'above' us. But human beings have to use picture-language when they are talking about God. Paul was using language which worshippers have used for a very long time, e.g. 'I saw the Lord high and lifted up' (Isa. 6.1). He used it again in Colossians 3.1: 'If then you have been raised with Christ, seek the things that are above', i.e. the things that are eternal.

'Upward call' does not mean God telling someone that his life on earth is over.

Let those of us who are mature be thus minded (v. 15a): Who were the 'mature'? Some people think that Paul was referring to the baptized members of the Church who were growing in their faithfulness to Christ. But it seems more likely that he was mocking them and that he meant, 'There are some who are so puffed up that they think they are complete Christians, or are without sin, or have reached the end of the course already. These people should note what I have said. They have a long way to go before they reach their "prize".' Paul mocked his readers in the same way in 1 Corinthians 8.1, as people who thought they knew everything.

If in anything you are otherwise minded, God will reveal that also to you (v. 15b): i.e. if you do not agree with me, there is One who will guide you into all the truth, namely God (see John 16.13).

Christian teachers and visitors and preachers find encouragement in the fact that they are like the seventy disciples whom Jesus 'sent on ahead of him . . . into every place where he himself was about to come' (Luke 10.1). A teacher's main task is to prepare the way so that God's Spirit can come in. They prepare for an event, they do not complete it. It is God who will 'reveal'.

Only let us hold true to what we have attained (v. 16): Paul meant that all Christians have understood something about God and about themselves. It may only be a very small part of the whole truth. But if they put into practice ('holds true') that part which they have grasped they can grow in their understanding. 'Those who have will be given more' (Matt. 13.23, NEB).

A Church member complained to her minister that she could not understand or believe every sentence in the Creed. He said, 'What *do* you understand?' She said, 'The first six words: "I believe in God the Father".' He said, 'Then treat God as your Father. Trust Him and talk freely with Him. And treat all men and women as your brothers and sisters. If you really do that you will see the reason for other parts of the Creed.'

The Greek word translated 'hold true' really refers to a group of people standing in line. So Paul was thinking of the whole congregation (and of its need for unity), not of any one separate individual.

STUDY SUGGESTIONS

WORDS

1. 'The Greek word translated "perfect" does not mean "absolutely good"' (p. 96).
   (a) What does it mean?
   (b) By what other English word is it also translated in Phil. 3.12–16?

CONTENT

2. 'Paul wrote these verses to prevent the Philippians from misunderstanding vv 2–11 . . . A reader might think that Paul was satisfied with his own life as a Christian' (p. 96).
   What did Paul do to prevent his readers from thinking that?
3. 'Forgetting what lies behind' (v. 13c).
   (a) Why did Paul want to forget?
   (b) Why is it more important for a Christian to look forward to the future rather than back to the past?
   (c) When Christians do look back to the past, what should they do about it?

BIBLE

4. In 3.12–14 Paul used the language of the Greek Games in order to illustrate his teaching. What sort of Games or athletics do the writers refer to in each of the following passages?
   (a) 1 Cor. 9.26   (b) Gal. 2.2   (c) Phil. 2.16
   (d) 2 Tim. 4.7, 8   (e) Heb. 12.1, 2
5. 'The upward call of God' (v. 14). What do we chiefly learn about God's 'call' from each of the following verses?

(a) Luke 5.32   (b) John 1.42   (c) John 3.16   (d) 1 Tim. 1.12
(e) Heb. 3.1   (f) Heb. 3.7.

DISCUSSION AND RESEARCH

6. 'Not that I am already perfect' (v.12a).
   (a) In what ways does your Church help its members to become 'mature'?
   (b) Are there any ways in which it hinders them from maturing?
7. 'One thing I do' (v. 13b).
   (a) What was the 'one thing' which Paul said that he did?
   (b) What do you yourself aim at doing above everything else?
8. 'Christians need to have a clear goal . . . it is important to learn from God the ways in which He wants them to grow and develop' (pp 97, 99). How does a Christian set about deciding what his goal should be? How does a congregation discover the directions in which God wants His Church to grow and develop?
9. 'People often say that it is better to live a Christian life because you love Christ than because you hope for a reward' (p. 100). Which do you think is better, and why?
10. 'I watched the pig-farmers at work for many months before I could usefully preach the gospel to them' (p. 100).
    (a) Why did the preacher have to do that?
    (b) In your experience, how far is it necessary for a minister to understand the occupations of those to whom he ministers?
11. 'Upward call' (v. 14) . . . 'Human beings have to use "picture-language" when they are talking about God' (p. 101).
    (a) Why do you think that people talk about God being 'up above'?
    (b) To what extent is it equally true to say that God is 'within' or 'underneath' or 'around' us? Deuteronomy 4.7; 7.21; 33.27 and John 15.5 may help you to think about this question.
12. Paul said that he pressed on 'for the prize of the upward call of God' (v. 14). One student understood this to mean that only very well-trained and mature Christians can receive the 'prize' of being 'called by God'.
    What is your own understanding of this verse?

3.17—4.1
Waiting for Christ's Coming

INTRODUCTION

Paul's thoughts were as follows:

1. You need examples to follow in order to live as Christians. Use us as your examples (v. 17).

2. I say this because there are guides who may lead you astray, guides who are concerned only for the things of this visible world (vv 18, 19).

3. But we Christians live in two worlds; this visible world and the invisible world where Christ is acknowledged as Lord. It is Christ who will transform us so that we experience the power of His life (vv 20, 21).

4. Therefore stand firm (4.1).

NOTES AND INTERPRETATION

Brethren, join in imitating me, and mark those who so live as you have an example in us (v. 17): i.e. 'Brethren, agree together in imitating me, and study all of us who live in this way. You have us as an example.' Paul meant, the Spirit of peace and joy which God gave to me He is offering to you also. Open yourselves to Him! It is not by magic that some people have peace and joy while others lack them.

Brethren, join . . .: Paul was again begging the Philippians to behave as a united congregation: 'join'. A strong congregation is one where, although members hold different opinions, the congregation as a whole shares the same aims.

Imitating:

(a) Whom should they imitate? This is the important question. Paul knew that the Philippians would follow the example of someone or other (as we all do). The question was, 'Whose example?' Paul's answer was, 'The example you see in myself and my colleagues, Epaphroditus and Timothy and others.'

(b) Why should Christians imitate other Christians? Chiefly because being a Christian concerns the way in which we live. What most other people want to know about Christians is not 'Are your ideas true?' but 'Can you *live* what you believe?' For human beings cannot learn about living except from seeing how other people live. In places where there has been a Church for a long time, traditions grow up concerning the way in which Christians should live, and from these traditions Christians receive some guidance. Parents hand down to their children the customs which they received from their parents, and the children do not fully realize that that is happening. But where the Church is young (as the Church in Philippi was), and where there are very few traditions, it is especially important for members to watch ('mark') living people. So Paul told his readers to watch him and his colleagues to see that it was indeed possible to live as Christians.

(c) What did Paul want them to imitate? He did not want them to copy everything he did, but to follow the way in which he lived, the way in which he faced persecution and hardship, the way in which he relied on the Spirit of Jesus Christ.

(d) How can a Christian be an example without becoming conceited? Paul has shown us three ways.

1. 'Follow my example as I follow Christ's' (1 Cor. 11.1, NEB); that is, 'We all need to follow the same example, namely that of Christ.'

2. 'Not that I have already obtained' (Phil. 3.12); that is 'I am still a learner.'

3. 'Those who so live', i.e. there are others as well as myself whose example you should follow. It has been said that a Pharisee's attitude to other religious teachers was 'I represent God: you do not.' This was no longer Paul's attitude towards his colleagues.

Live: The Greek word here translated 'live' means 'walk', and is often translated 'walk'. In the Old and New Testaments 'walking' refers to the sort of life we live, the way we behave. It also refers to the fact that believers have a goal towards which they are travelling: we walk in order to get somewhere. 'Walk in the law of the Lord' (Ps. 119.1). 'This is the way, walk in it' (Isa. 30.21). 'Walk in newness of life' (Rom. 6.4).

Many . . . live as enemies of the cross of Christ (v. 18): In 3.2–11 Paul warned his readers against those who wanted them to return to Jewish ways. But in v. 18 he referred to a different group of people.

These were not enemies of Christ Himself, but of His 'cross'. They had refused to accept the way in which Christ had done His work: they refused to accept persecution and suffering. They regarded the Church as the place where they ought to receive comfort and support. They were unhappy to belong to a Church whose sign was a cross of death, and in which belonging meant suffering.

Their end is destruction, their god is the belly, and they glory in their shame (v. 19a): No one is sure who these people were, of whom Paul said that their 'end was destruction'. They may have been a group of Christians who had wrongly interpreted his teaching about 'freedom'. Paul wrote, for example, in Romans 7.6: 'Now we are discharged from the law.' As a result there were some who thought that they could reject all rules and discipline and responsibility. They said, 'Live as you please and God will always forgive and forget' (see Rom. 6.15).

Or they may have been Christians who had been influenced by the Greek philosophers called 'Gnostics'. Some of these philosophers taught that the human spirit was good, but that all material things (including the human body) were evil. Therefore people could do whatever they liked with their bodies and their possessions.

Their end: Paul was always concerned with what would happen to himself and to other people 'in the end' (as we shall see in v. 21a). He sometimes compared this 'end' to the end of a race (see 3.13, 14). Perhaps in this verse he had in mind a runner who finished the race but collapsed at the finishing post.

Destruction: See note on 1.28.

Their god is the belly: We saw in the note on v. 18 that there were people who rejected Christ's way of suffering. In this verse Paul added something else about them: their greed. 'Greed' does not refer only to eating and drinking too much. A 'greedy' person is one who: (a) lives as if it was more important to increase his possessions than to increase his awareness of God; (b) tries to increase his possessions without thinking of other people's needs; (c) becomes richer by making other people poorer; (d) forgets that the 'earth is the Lord's' (Ps. 24.1), and forgets that he is answerable to God for the way in which he uses the good things of the earth. He cuts down God's trees without planting new ones, he uses God's oil wastefully, and pollutes God's air and water.

Glory in: See note on 3.3b.

Minds . . . set on earthly things (v. 19b): Paul did not despise earthly things. In 1.24 and 2.15 we see that he fully accepted the duties of living in this world, and the importance of obeying the laws of the Roman Empire. But he was also a citizen of an invisible world (see 3.14 and note on 3.20).

The people to whom Paul referred here would only trust the things of this world, things they could know through the senses of their physical body. Only the things which they could touch or smell or hear or taste or measure were real to them. So it became impossible for them to trust the invisible God.

But our commonwealth is in heaven (v. 20a) (NEB: *'We are citizens of heaven';* Moffatt: *'We are a colony of heaven'):* The word 'common-wealth' means the region to which we belong, the region of which we, along with others, are citizens.

Here is more language which (like the references to the Games in vv 12–16) the Philippian Christians could well understand. Philippi was a Roman colony (Acts 16.12). In its population were many old Roman soldiers who had been rewarded by being made full citizens of the Empire and by being given houses in this colony. In their speech and dress and morals they behaved just as they would have done if they had been living in Rome. (Similarly after World War I the British Government encouraged demobilized soldiers to settle with their families in countries which were then parts of the Empire, such as Kenya and Canada.)

Paul himself was a full Roman citizen. When he was visiting Philippi he was imprisoned without a trial, and was only released when the magistrates learned that he was a Roman citizen (Acts 16.38).

In v. 20a Paul was saying: 'Just as a Roman citizen living in Philippi never forgets that he belongs to the great Roman Empire, do not forget that you also belong to an even greater empire which is "heaven".' A West African proverb says: 'The world is our market, heaven is our home.' Of course we owe loyalty to the authorities on earth; but we also belong to the invisible empire, of which the eternal God is the head. We owe loyalty to Him, and by Him we are inspired and supported. For similar teaching see Ephesians 2.19, 'You are fellow-citizens with the saints and members of the household of God.'

All Christians owe this same sort of 'double loyalty'. There are times when it does not seem possible to fulfil both loyalties, and we have to decide how to put first the 'commonwealth of heaven'.

In one of the very small African states it is the Churches which have provided most of the education. As a result nearly all the national leaders are members of the Church, although 95 per cent of the people are Muslims. As this is being written, the last President has just died. The only candidates for the Presidency are both Christians, but they are in a difficult position. They know that whoever is elected will be expected to become a Muslim in order to keep the confidence of the Muslims. They also know that if neither of them stands for election, a pro-Communist candidate will be elected.

Heaven:

1. In some places in the Bible 'heaven' simply means 'the sky'. 'Taking the five loaves . . . he looked up to heaven' (Luke 9.16).

2. Many people thought of God as being in one place rather than in another, and thought of the sky as that place. 'He who sits in the heavens laughs' (Psalm 2.4).

3. The Jews, through reverence for God, did not want to use His name and often used the word 'heaven' when they meant 'God', e.g. 'Father, I have sinned against heaven' (Luke 15.18).

4. The chief teaching of the New Testament writers about God is that He is Spirit (John 4.24), and therefore does not live in any one place. Thus 'heaven' is not a place. It is fellowship with the eternal and invisible God. When God meets man and man meets God, that is

heaven. See Matthew 18.4: 'Whoever humbles himself . . . is the greatest in the kingdom of heaven.'

5. Heaven is for us now, not a gift which God gives us after we die. John's purpose in the Book of Revelation was not to describe life after death. He was giving us in symbolic language his vision of the triumph of God over evil. 'War arose in heaven, Michael and his angels fighting against the dragon: and the dragon and his angels fought, but they were defeated' (Rev. 12. 7, 8).

From it we await a Saviour, the Lord Jesus Christ (v. 20b):
From it: Paul, having referred to God's invisible empire, heaven, now added that it was from God Himself that salvation would come. This is one more phrase in which he made it clear that salvation is a gift from God, and not something which human beings can produce or can earn for themselves.

We await: i.e. full salvation is a gift which we shall one day receive. It is true that when a Christian has accepted God's offer to rescue him from the overwhelming power of his sins we can say that he 'has been' saved (Eph. 2.8). But Paul often emphasized that this salvation needed to be completed. In 1 Corinthians 1.18 he wrote about 'us who are being saved'. See above, note on Philippians 3.12b. So we 'await' a Saviour.

We should note that Paul was not writing about the salvation of individuals at the time of their death, but about 'the end', i.e. the time when Jesus would be finally victorious over all evil (see Acts 3.21: 'Jesus must be received into heaven until the time of universal restoration', NEB).

A saviour: Paul hardly ever used this word when he was referring to Jesus. The reason for this is probably that at that time people often used the word to describe an emperor or a military leader who, by the use of armies, defeated a national enemy. Or they used the word to describe some individual who rescued the country from chaos by overthrowing the existing ruler by a 'coup'. It was because Jesus used other means than force that Paul did not usually call him 'Saviour'. Jesus reconciled us to God ('saved' us) by dying on the cross, and brings us to a completed salvation by living in us. 'If while we were enemies we were reconciled to God by the death of his Son, much more, now that we are reconciled, shall we be saved by his life' (Rom. 5.10). See also note on Philippians 2.12 about 'salvation'.

The Lord: See note on 2.11a.

Who will change our lowly body to be like his glorious body (v. 21a): As we have seen (p. 106) Paul was deeply concerned with the events that would take place at the end of time. He did not claim that he knew what would happen or that he could prove what he said. He was able to write about God's actions in the future only because of what he knew about God's actions in the past. God had sent Jesus so that through

Him human beings were able to have fellowship with God. But, Paul said, God would not have done this unless He had a purpose for the whole of His creation in the future. The teaching of this verse, then, concerns what will happen to Christians 'at the end of all things', rather than at the death of the body (see note on 1.6b).

Who will change: God will change, not annihilate, people's 'bodies', so that they can have a different way of expressing themselves (see note below on 'body'). Greek philosophers taught that at death the 'body' was destroyed and the 'soul' survived. But Hebrew thinkers refused to split the 'body' from the 'soul': they regarded a person as a whole person. Therefore Paul wrote that God would change or transform 'the body', not destroy it.

Our lowly body: that is, the body which is powerless in so many ways, the body which becomes ill and decays. Paul himself probably suffered from some bodily illness which he called his 'thorn in his flesh' (2 Cor. 12.7). He knew the ways in which his body prevented him from doing what he wanted to do. But nowhere did he ever call the body 'evil'.

The AV translation 'vile' is very misleading.

To be like his glorious body: that is, to share the power and the freedom of Christ's risen life. The phrase 'his glorious body' shows clearly that 'body' does not mean flesh and blood.

Readers sometimes ask what sort of existence there is between death and this final moment of being 'like his glorious body'. For a discussion of this question see note on 1.23b, p. 38.

Body:

1. In the Bible the word 'body' sometimes means the flesh and bones of a person. 'Do not fear those who kill the body but cannot kill the soul' (Matt. 10.28; also Matt. 6.25).

2. Although this physical body suffers weakness, and decay ('It is sown in dishonour . . . it is sown in weakness' 1 Cor. 15.43), it is in its nature good, not evil. Jesus did not regard the physical body as evil. Nor did Christians, until some of them were led astray by religious groups from Asia, such as the 3rd century 'Manichaeans'.

3. But 'body' usually means 'a person'. As we have seen, writers in the Bible did not regard the 'body' as separate from the whole 'self' or personality. 'Present your bodies as a living sacrifice' (Rom. 12.1) means 'Present yourselves'. Paul wrote: 'He who joins himself to a prostitute becomes one body with her . . . the two shall become one' (1 Cor. 6.16); that is, sexual union is not simply the union of two physical bodies but of two personalities.

4. Paul taught that the 'natural body' (the flesh and bones) ceases, and that God changes it into another sort of body. He called it a 'spiritual body' (1 Cor. 15.44). It is called the 'resurrection of the

body' in the Creeds. 'Body' thus means the means by which a person expresses himself.

5. Paul also used the word to refer to the Church, because it is the means by which Christ expresses himself in the world. 'You are the body of Christ' (1 Cor. 12.27).

By the power which enables him even to subject all things to himself (v. 21b):

The power: Here again we see how different were the beliefs of Greek philosophers and Paul's beliefs. First, the Greeks taught that human beings are by nature immortal, that their 'souls' endure for ever. Paul taught that life after death (and sharing God's life at the end of time) is due to the power of God, it is his gift. Secondly, the Greeks taught that gods exist but take no action in human affairs. But Paul (like all writers in the Bible) believed that God had 'power' and took action in the world (see note on 3.10a). 'Power' is the word Jesus used when the Sadducees told a story in order to ridicule the belief in life after death. He said, 'You know neither the scriptures nor the power of God' (Mark 12.24).

Subject all things: Paul must have brought great hope to his readers by writing this. They were living in a city where the forces of evil seemed much stronger than the forces of good. They were being persecuted, and the persecutors seemed more powerful than the Christians. Then Paul said: 'But in the end God will be victorious over all evil.'

Therefore, my brethren, whom I love and long for, my joy and crown, stand firm thus in the Lord (4.1): 'Therefore' means 'Because we have such a glorious time ahead of us'.

Love and long for: These words remind us of the suffering which Paul endured in his imprisonment, cut off from his friends.

My joy and crown: In 3.12–16 Paul had referred to athletes who took part in the Games and who hoped to receive the 'prize' or 'crown'. Here he compared himself to a runner who had the 'joy' of receiving the 'crown' from the hands of Christ, and the crown was the Philippian congregation. (How many ministers can see their congregation as a prize given to them by Christ?)

Stand firm thus in Lord: There were very many temptations into which the Philippians might fall, and Paul had referred to some of them in Chapter 3. They might follow the example of the 'dogs' (3.2) who were trying to persuade them to return to the old Jewish ways, and might make the keeping of regulations take the place of personal loyalty to God himself. They might imitate those who thought that they were 'mature' and had no more to learn (3.15). They might refuse to accept the suffering which came to all faithful Christians, and might fall into despair, and use the Church only as a place of consolation. (3.18). Or they might be so much concerned with the things of this world that they forgot that they belonged to the invisible kingdom of God (3.20a).

It was in order to help them to stand firm against temptations like these that Paul wrote this verse. He wanted them to stand 'in the Lord' (see note on 4.10), i.e. to keep the company not only of each other, but of Jesus Christ himself.

STUDY SUGGESTIONS

WORDS

1. Why did Paul so rarely use the word 'Saviour' when he referred to Jesus?
2. What meaning do people give the word 'heaven' when they use it in ordinary conversation? (See Questions 8 and 10 below).

CONTENT

3. What was Paul's chief teaching about the 'body' (i.e. our physical form):
   (a) during life on earth?
   (b) after death?
4. Why did Paul say that he 'longed for' the Philippians?
5. Paul exhorted the Philippians to 'stand firm in the Lord' (4.1).
   (a) Against whom or what, according to Philippians 2 and 3, did they need to stand firm? (Give references.)
   (b) In what way might Paul's words in 3.21b help them to do this?

BIBLE

6. The Greek word which is translated 'live' in v. 17 means 'walk'. How is it translated in each of the following passages, (i) in a modern translation, (ii) in another language which you know?
   (a) John 8.12   (b) John 12.35   (c) Galatians 5.16
   (d) Ephesians 2.2   (e) 1 John 1.6, 7   (f) 1 John 2.6
7. Which verse in this section of the letter contains a truth which we also find in the following three passages?
   Colossians 3.2,3   Hebrews 11.13–16   1 Peter 2.11
8. Read again the study on the word 'heaven' (pp. 107, 108). Which of the various meanings listed there would you understand by the word 'heaven' in each of the following passages?
   (a) Matt. 5.16   (b) Matt. 16.19   (c) Matt. 23.13
   (d) Mark 8.11   (e) John 17.1   (f) Heb. 11.12   (g) 1 Peter 1.12
   (h) Revelation 18.5

DISCUSSION AND RESEARCH

9. Paul exhorted the Philippians to 'imitate' his example and that of his fellow-workers (v. 17).

111

(a) Why should Christians imitate other Christians? In what ways, if any, should they *not* imitate other Christians?

(b) Some Christians find it helpful to hear and read about the lives of saints and heroes in the history of the Church. Others become depressed, feeling that such examples are too high for them to follow. What is your own feeling about trying to imitate great Christians of the past?

(c) Whom do the young men and women whom you know imitate today?

10. Whom did Paul mean by 'enemies of the cross of Christ' (3.18)? Whom do you see as the 'enemies of the cross of Christ' today? In discussing this question remember that Paul referred to these people 'with tears'. Why did he do so?

11. 'Their god is the belly' (3.19). 'Greed does not refer only to eating and drinking too much' (p. 106).

(a) What other sorts of greed do Christians chiefly need to beware of today?

(b) How can they resist temptations to be 'greedy'?

12. 'In v. 20a Paul was saying, "A Roman citizen belongs to the Roman Empire . . . you also belong to an even greater empire, which is heaven." All Christians owe this sort of "double loyalty". At times it does not seem possible to fulfil both loyalties' (p. 107).

(a) Give an example of Christians finding that their loyalty to God conflicts with their loyalty to their country. What was the outcome?

(b) Read again the paragraph on p. 107 about an election to an African Presidency. What action do you think a Christian candidate should take? Give reasons for your answer.

13. Philippians 3.12–21 is sometimes read at funeral services (often with vv 7–11 as well). How suitable do you think this passage is for a funeral? Give your reasons.

4.2–9

God Offers us His Peace

INTRODUCTION

In this paragraph Paul seems to have been replying to a piece of bad news which he had received from Philippi. Two women, both leading members of the congregation, had had a serious quarrel. Instead of simply replying, 'Don't quarrel,' Paul wrote a paragraph full of positive encouragement. It is in three parts:

1. An urgent appeal for peace (vv 2, 3).
2. Some ways in which peace comes:
    (a) Let your joy come from being in the Lord (v. 4),
    (b) Let others know you as forbearing people (v. 5a),
    (c) God has the future under control (v. 5b),
    (d) Therefore don't be anxious (v. 6a),
    (e) Say your prayers whatever happens (v. 6b),
    (f) Asking God and thanking God (v. 6b),
    (g) In this way you will receive God's peace (v. 7).
3. (An extra note) The importance of looking for and valuing goodness, in everyone whom you meet (vv 8, 9).

NOTES AND INTERPRETATION

I entreat Euodia and Syntyche to agree in the Lord (v. 2):
Euodia and Syntyche: We do not read about these two anywhere else, but it is clear from v. 3 that they were women and that they were good and sincere Christian workers in Philippi. Why had they quarrelled? Paul has not told us, but perhaps each one felt that what she did for the congregation, and the gifts that God had given her, made her superior to the other. Then, probably, members of the congregation took sides, and so a serious division existed. Something like this has happened in most Christian congregations. What can be done about it?
Agree in the Lord: This division could be healed if they agreed 'in the Lord' (see note on 4.10a). This did not mean that they ought to have the same ideas or convictions or feelings. Each Christian is distinctive from other Christians, and each has his or her own distinctive contribution to make to the congregation. It meant that they could find peace:
    (a) By fixing their attention on the Lord (rather than on themselves);
    (b) By recognizing their own weakness and sinfulness, and their need for His forgiveness;
    (c) By attending to the aims which the Lord had put before them (rather than on the ways of achieving those aims). See notes on 1.27; 2.3; and 2.5.
I ask you, also, true yokefellow, help these women (v. 3a):
I ask you: Paul did not issue a command, just as he did not command the women to agree. He begged them to help each other to heal their divisions, because he loved them and was concerned about them.
Yokefellow: Who was the person whom Paul addressed like this?
Either he was a member of the congregation who had once worked with Paul in Philippi, *or* his name was Syzygos (which means 'yokefellow' or 'true comrade').

Help: Paul did not ask him to insist that the two women should work in harmony, but to stand alongside them so that they could themselves find it. That is 'helping'.

These women: There are many references in Acts to the important part which women played in the Church in that district of Greece. See Acts 17.4: 'not a few of the leading women', and 17.12: 'Greek women of high standing'. See also Acts 16.13–14. The position of women in Philippi was probably higher than in most Greek cities because Philippi was a Roman colony. In Rome women were often influential in society. So it is not surprising to read of women being prominent in the Church at Philippi.

Those who read this may ask, 'Is our Church today giving women full opportunity to serve God in the Church?' In places where the Church does not give women such opportunity, there may be good reasons for this. For example, in some cultures it is not the custom for a woman to take a leading part in any public events. A woman who did so would be regarded as 'immoral'. This is probably the reason why Paul said that it was 'shameful' for a woman to speak in church (1 Cor. 14.35).

But sometimes the reasons for excluding women from positions of responsibility are not good, e.g. if the reason is simply that people do not want changes of any sort, or the men in the congregation want to dictate to the women.

This is not an easy problem for Churches to solve. They face the question, 'To what extent should the Church lead the rest of society, and to what extent should it accept the present conventions of society?'

For they have laboured side by side with me in the gospel (v. 3b): The words mean much more than 'laboured'. Better translations would be, 'They have fought at my side in defending the gospel', or 'They have been united with me in preaching the gospel in the face of opposition.' The congregation to which Paul wrote this letter was, as we have seen, a tiny minority living amongst neighbours of whom many were against them.

Whose names are in the book of life (v. 3c): Greek cities had a register of their citizens, as some modern cities have. So in several passages in the New Testament those who accept the sovereignty of God are mentioned as having their names 'in the book'. See Luke 10.20: 'Rejoice that your names are written in heaven.' Here Paul meant that God had accepted their work and made their work a part of His own.

Some readers, having studied passages in Revelation, point to the fact that there are people whose names are *not* in the 'book of life'. See Revelation 20.15: 'If anyone's name was not found written in the book of life, he was thrown into the lake of fire.' We should note therefore that it is indeed possible to deprive ourselves of God's fellowship, and to experience the agony of separation.

We may note that the author of Revelation added that there were those 'whose names have not been written in the book of life from the foundation of the world' (Rev. 17.8); i.e. that God created some people to be for ever separated from Him. This is teaching which bodies such as Jehovah's Witnesses have made into one of the foundations of their creed. But we do not find evidence for this in the New Testament as a whole. See Matthew 18.14: 'It is not the will of my Father that one of these little ones should perish,' and 2 Peter 3.9: 'The Lord is forbearing toward you, not wishing that any should perish, but that all should reach repentance.' One reason why God's Church has been divided is that Christians have sometimes based their beliefs on a single verse or passage in the Bible, instead of basing it on the New Testament as a whole.

Rejoice in the Lord always (v. 4): This can be translated: 'Farewell; I wish you all joy in the Lord' (NEB), but it is more likely that it means; 'May you always be joyful as you live your life in the Lord.' ('Always' means 'in all circumstances'.)

Rejoice: What is 'joy' and who are the 'joyful' people?

1. Rejoicing is not the same as smiling or laughing or joking or singing, although a joyful Christian may often do these things.

2. A joyful person does not depend on success or popularity or possessions or any other outward circumstances, although he may sometimes have them. If he cannot rejoice unless things are going well, then he has not yet learnt how to 'rejoice in the Lord'. See Romans 14.17: 'The kingdom of God does not mean food and drink but . . . joy in the Holy Spirit.'

3. The joyful people of whom Paul wrote rejoiced 'in the Lord'. They became joyful because they lived in the presence of God and were in fellowship with Him and were able to receive His joy ('That my joy may be in you', John 15.11). They were convinced that God is good ('Make a joyful noise . . . for the Lord is good', Psalm 100.1, 5).

4. For this reason a Christian can be 'joyful' even while he is suffering or being persecuted for the sake of Christ. The suffering does not destroy the joy. So St Polycarp could say as they prepared to kill him (about AD 155): 'I thank you, Father, that you have judged me worthy of this hour.' So Paul was able to write joyfully to the Philippians although he was in prison and might soon be killed. See Luke 6.22, 23: 'Blessed are you when men hate you . . . on account of the Son of man! Rejoice in that day, and leap for joy.' This joy is like the sea water that is perfectly still in the deep places even though there may be great and dangerous waves on the surface.

5. Joy is something which God intends us to share with one another: 'Rejoice with those who rejoice' (Rom. 12.15). A Christian shows generosity in his rejoicing by looking away from himself to what God is

doing for other people: 'While your obedience is known to all . . . I rejoice' (Rom. 16.19).

6. Although God gives us joy in this life, we shall not experience it fully until we are fully in fellowship with God. Revelation 19 is a vision of that future time: 'Hallelujah! For the Lord . . . reigns. Let us rejoice and exult' (Rev. 19.6, 7).

Other references in this letter to 'rejoicing' are: 1.18, 19; 2.17,18; 2.28; 3.1; 4.10.

Let all men know your forbearance: (v. 5a):

Forbearance: It is not easy to find a word to translate the Greek word which Paul used. Some translators have unfortunately used words like 'moderation' (AV), which many people interpret as meaning inactive or weak. We may see its meaning by describing people who have 'forbearance'. They are ready to believe that they may be mistaken, they do not always insist on their rights, they are considerate and gentle to others, they are ready to forgive others and to be forgiven by them, they are generous in praising others and merciful in judging them, they are more keen to turn their opponents into friends than to attack them. They are not obstinate or stiff in mind or resentful. 'If anyone forces you to go one mile, go with him two miles. Give to him who begs from you, and do not refuse him who would borrow from you' (Matt. 5.41, 42).

Let all men know: Paul hoped that when people talked about the Christians in Philippi they would say, 'They have a name for being "forbearing",' just as when they talked about the Romans they said, 'They have a name for being good administrators'. He was not encouraging them to boast about themselves, but urging them to represent Christ faithfully. See Matthew 5.16: 'Let your light so shine before men that they may give glory to your Father.'

Those outside the Church, therefore, will always find out what it means to be a Christian by watching the behaviour of Christians. This is true whether Christians and non-Christians live peaceably together (as generally happens), or whether there is active persecution of the Church (as is happening in many places as this is being written). When a non-Christian comes to a Church official in order, for example, to discuss the boundary between his property and the Church property, or to complain about excessive noise at night during a Christian festival, or to accuse him of disloyalty to the State, he either sees or fails to see the signs of Christlike living, of which forbearance is one.

The Lord is at hand (v. 5b):

(a) This probably means: 'The Lord will soon return.' If so, then this is the fifth time in this letter that Paul referred to the 'coming', or 'day' of Jesus (see note on 1.6). So v. 5 means, 'Be forbearing and don't repay evil for evil, because Jesus is coming to be the judge of everyone.' Just as travellers walking throughout the day look forward to the time when they have reached their goal, so Paul looked forward to the day of Christ. So he prayed, 'Our Lord, come!' (1 Cor. 16.22).

(b) But some people think that it means: 'The Lord is always present or near at hand' (as in Psalm 119.151: 'Thou art near, O Lord'). If this is what Paul meant, then the meaning is 'You can bear suffering and persecution because the Lord is alongside you and with you.'

Have no anxiety (v. 6):

1. The Greek word which is translated 'anxiety' is like the English word 'care'. Sometimes it means 'loving attention', e.g. in Paul's 'anxiety for all churches' (2 Cor. 11.28). See also note on 2.20. Here and in many other passages it means 'worry'. (The AV translation, 'be careful for nothing', is misleading today because to most people that means, 'Don't take trouble', 'Don't make preparations').

2. Concerning 'anxiety' Jesus said that we have to make a choice. The choice is between trusting chiefly in what we ourselves can do, and trusting chiefly in what God can do. An anxious Christian, He said, is like someone trying to serve two employers at the same time. 'No one can serve two masters . . . Therefore I tell you, do not be anxious about your life' (Matt. 6.24, 25).

3. Jesus spoke of those who are anxious about the present: 'Do not be anxious about what you shall eat, nor about your body, what you shall put on' (Matt. 6.25). He also spoke of those who were anxious about the future, for example those who were worried about what they should say if they were persecuted: 'When they bring you to trial . . . do not be anxious beforehand what you are to say' (Mark 13.11).

Note that none of the NT writers teach that Christians should forget about feeding and clothing themselves and their families, or that they should refrain from making plans for the future. What they teach is 'Do not make your plans in such a way that you trust God less'.

4. How can we get rid of anxiety? In the next sentence Paul answered this question: he said 'By praying'. By praying we turn our attention to God's love and His power, rather than to ourselves. We realize each time that His love and His power are greater than our needs.

This was the experience of Y. D. Tiwari, a Hindu, who was deeply anxious about himself. He describes what happened when he was 22: 'The more I struggled the more I sank. . . . Then in a time of silence I read Christ's words "Ask·in my name" . . . But I was horrified at the thought of doing so. I was a Brahmin . . . But I was face to face with the Lord. I had tried to be saved by this philosophy and meditation and it had not worked . . . So I got up from my chair and knelt there and prayed. "O Lord if you are a living Lord save me from myself." And at once I realized there was a gracious personality by my side on whom I might rest my feverish head."

But in everything by prayer and supplication with thanksgiving let your requests be made known to God (v. 6b):

In everything: Whatever the Philippian Christians were worried about, whatever they were hoping for or fearing, whether they were experiencing pain or pleasure, they could take it to God by praying to Him.

By prayer and supplication: The word translated '*prayer*' means prayer of all sorts. It is placing ourselves as we really are in God's presence. It is letting his authority challenge us. It is letting His love surround us as we rediscover each time that God is to us as a father is to his children. We may be alone or with others. We may be silent or speak aloud. We may put prayer into words or pray without words. When we are in great pain our prayer may be, 'Lord, I cannot pray.' We may sit or stand or kneel or lie still.

The words '*supplication*' and '*requests*' mean one sort of prayer, namely the prayer of asking. Asking may be for our own needs, or it may be for the needs of others. In this sort of prayer:

(a) We are showing that we depend upon God. We are not like the Stoics of Paul's time who said, 'We are not affected by circumstances. We have no need of help.'

(b) We tell God without any pretence or holding back what we and others need.

(c) We do not only pray for His help for the world in general, but we make particular requests: 'Take away my pain.' 'Show us how to heal this quarrel.' This was the teaching which Jesus gave in his parable of the man who asked his friend to lend him some bread at midnight (see Luke 11.5–13).

(d) But we leave the result of our asking in God's hands. We often (though not always) know what we *want*. But He knows far better than we do what we *need*. So we sum up all our asking prayers in the words, 'Thy will be done' (Matt. 6.10).

With thanksgiving: These words are connected with the words 'in everything', i.e. be thankful whatever happens. Once again we need to remember that Paul was in prison when he wrote this, and that his readers were living in very difficult circumstances. His teaching was that, whatever happens, God's love for us is continuing and totally reliable, and that this is what we can be thankful for in all circumstances. 'We know that in everything God works for good with those who love Him' (Rom. 8.28).

But this kind of thanksgiving is not something we are born with. It is possible for us only if we have discovered how to use our suffering in the

'Have no anxiety about anything' (4.6).

Is it really possible for us to follow this guidance which Paul gives? What could have enabled this political prisoner in South-East Asia, being interrogated by the authorities, to be without anxiety? In what verses did Paul answer these questions? How far do his words satisfy you?

right way. A nurse from West Germany who was visiting Pakistan looked after a Christian boy who was slowly recovering from stab wounds. She said, 'I learnt from him, in a way I had not learnt anywhere else, what gratitude is.' Another nurse, who works in Northern Nigeria, wrote, 'The most grateful and joyful person in our hospital is the blind evangelist.'

In the 1939–45 war two Dutch Christian sisters helped Jewish people to escape from the Nazis. When this was discovered the Nazis put them into prison, into a place which had room for 400 prisoners but into which 1,400 had been crowded. They suffered not only from starvation, but from the smell and dirt and noise and fleas. One night one of the Dutch women read 1 Thessalonians 5.18: 'Give thanks in all circumstances.' Her sister said, 'We can't give thanks here.' The other said 'We can! We can give thanks that our Father is in heaven, that we are still together, that there are so many people in this place that they cannot avoid hearing about Jesus as you and I talk together. And we can thank God for the fleas.' Her sister said, 'No! We cannot thank God for the fleas!' 'We can,' said the other. 'There are so many of them that the guards will stay away and will not come to ill-treat us!' (This story comes from *The Hiding Place* by Corrie Ten Boom.)

Be made known to God: Christians 'make known' their needs to God, not because He requires the information, but because they are sharing their whole lives with Him if they are 'in the Lord' (v. 10). A small boy who is ill may say to his mother, 'It hurts, Mother,' and she may say, 'I know it hurts, my child.' The child has not told his mother anything she did not know, but is comforted by having shared his pain with his mother.

The peace of God, which passes all understanding, will keep your hearts and your minds in Christ Jesus (v. 7): In this verse Paul taught that, in the dangers and temptations of life, the Philippians were not alone. God was 'for' them (Rom. 8.31).

The peace of God: i.e. the peace which God gives. What is 'peace'?

1. In a few passages in the Bible 'peace' means 'absence of conflict', e.g. Acts 12.20: 'King Herod was angry with the people of Tyre and Sidon; and they came to him . . . and asked for peace because their country depended on the king's country for food.' But see note 4 below.

2. Often it is a greeting (e.g. in Phil. 1.2; Luke 10.5; etc.), just as the words for peace, '*Salaam*', '*Shalom*', etc., in many modern languages are greetings.

3. Usually it means a gift which God gives to mankind. Sometimes it is called 'God's' peace (as in this verse and in v. 9). Occasionally it is called 'Christ's', e.g. 'Let the peace of Christ rule in your hearts (Col. 3.15); 'My peace I give to you' (John 14.27).

4. This gift is a 'completeness' or 'wholeness' which comes to a group of people or to individuals when they are in a right relationship with other people. 'May the God of peace equip you with everything good that you may do His will' (Heb. 13.20).

5. A right relationship with God comes when we accept the forgiveness which He offers to us, and when we depend on His purposes rather than our own. 'Therefore, since we are justified by faith, we have peace with God through our Lord Jesus Christ' (Rom. 5.1).

A right relationship with other people comes when we are able to forgive them and to accept forgiveness from them (Eph. 4.3). But there can be real peace among Christians even when they disagree with one another, e.g. when they serve the same Lord, but by different methods. The Hebrew word '*shalom*', like the Hindi word '*santi*', means that sort of peace.

6. God calls on those who have received this gift of peace to share it with others, i.e. to be peacemakers (Matt. 5.9).

7. What writers in the Bible call 'peace' is different from what most people in the world call 'peace'. For most people 'peace' depends mainly on outside circumstances, e.g. the absence of noise or the absence of conflict. For writers in the Bible it comes from a right relationship with God. We see the peace that Jesus Himself had when we read the account of His trial by Pilate in John 19.5–14. Although, through Pilate's cowardice, Jesus was about to be condemned to death, it was Jesus, not Pilate, who had the peace of God.

Passes all understanding: means *either* 'Peace which is better than anything which we could create for ourselves', *or* 'Peace which gives us more than we had expected', *or* 'Peace which is so marvellous that we cannot understand why God has given it to us.'

Will keep: The Greeks used this word to describe a body of soldiers 'keeping guard' over a city, as the Romans kept guard over Philippi. (See 1 Peter 1.5: 'You, who by God's power are guarded through faith'.)

Your hearts and your minds: God will guard and protect their 'heart' (i.e. their feelings and their freedom of choice), and keep guard over their 'thoughts' (i.e. their intelligence).

In Christ Jesus: i.e. all this is true for someone who lives 'in Christ'. See note on 4.10a.

Whatever is true . . . honourable . . . just . . . pure . . . lovely . . . gracious . . . think about these things (v. 8): In other passages in this letter Paul wrote about the difference between Christians and other people. The Christians were set apart ('saints', 1.1); they shone out like stars on a dark night (2.15). But here Paul pointed to the goodness which God had given to people outside the Church as well as to themselves. All the words in this verse are words which Greeks and Romans of that time (who were not Christians) used in order to describe a 'good' person. As we have seen, most people in Philippi were Romans.

Like the Philippians, Christians in every generation need to behave as people 'set apart'. They are not 'of the world' (i.e. they do not follow the world as their guide). But God has placed them in the world (John 17.14) and in touch with the people of other religions (or of no religion) among whom they live. God intends them to notice and enjoy the various forms of goodness which He has given to His people everywhere. We recollect how Jesus said to the Canaanite woman, 'Great is your faith' (Matt. 15.28), and after meeting the Roman centurion, 'Not even in Israel have I found such faith' (Luke 7.9).

True: those who follow the truth as far as they can see it, rather than following what most people think or what is convenient to think.

Honourable: those who rightly earn respect from others.

Just: those who treat their fellow-men with fairness.

Pure: those who are single-minded and loyal, and not divided in their loyalties.

Lovely: those whom others love because of the goodness in their lives (it does not mean 'beautiful to look at').

Gracious: those whom others rightly speak well of.

Think about these things: By this Paul meant far more than 'Remember that there is this goodness in the world.' He meant, 'Make a point of noticing good people of this sort wherever they exist.' See 1.10: 'Approve what is excellent.'

Why is it important for Christians to do this:

(a) Christians grow in character by enjoying and being grateful for goodness, rather than by fixing their attention mainly on the evil in the world. We all tend to become what we most often see. This is why it is useful to think of good men and women, and especially of Christ Himself, when we meditate. (The newspapers and radio and television will provide enough news of the evil in the world!)

A man who had memorized the Beatitudes (Matt. 5.3–10) used to repeat them just before he went to sleep at night. In this way he fixed his mind on the goodness in the world, and especially on God's goodness (which is referred to in the second half of each verse).

(b) Christians learn that God is alive and at work throughout the world and not only in the Church. God 'did not leave himself without witness' (Acts 14.17).

(c) As Christians appreciate the goodness of non-Christians, they can grow in humility.

What you have learned and received and heard and seen in me, do (v. 9): It might seem that Paul was boasting in this verse. But this is not so. He was saying: 'What I have written above, about joy and forbearance and prayer and peace, is not just a collection of good ideas or theories. I was describing a life that a man can live, and it has been my responsibility to live it as best I can, and you have seen it. Now put it into practice.'

From the five verbs of this verse we see how he had taught the people at Philippi (and also how any good teacher does his work):

1. They '*learned*' because he taught them out of his experience.

2. They '*received*' because he also handed on the tradition of past Christians.

3. and 4. They had '*heard*' and '*seen*' because he practised what he taught.

5. They should '*do*'. He had a practical aim, i.e. that they should not only know what it means to be a Christian, they should also live it.

STUDY SUGGESTIONS

WORDS

1. 'Forbearance' (4.5).
   (a) How has this word been translated into another language which you know? What is the full meaning of that word? How good a translation is it?
   (b) Which 6 of the following words would you use to describe a person who has 'forbearance'?
   forgiving   overbearing   considerate   arrogant
   generous   gentle   inactive   meek   obstinate
   moderate   merciful

CONTENT

2. Two women workers in the Philippian congregation had had a serious quarrel. Paul entreated them to 'agree in the Lord'. List 3 ways in which he suggested that they could be helped to do so.
3. Express in your own words the truth which Paul declared in 4.2; and also in 1.27; 2.5 and 2.3.
4. What did Paul mean when he said that the names of his fellow-workers were 'in the book of life'? (v. 3).
5. 'What writers in the Bible call "peace" is different from what most people in the world call "peace"' (p. 121). How would you describe 'the peace of God' (v. 7.)?
6. What did Paul say about prayer in this passage?

BIBLE

7. What do we learn from this passage, and from the following verses, about the position of women in the Church in Paul's time?

Acts 16.13–14   Acts 17.4,12   Acts 18.26   Rom. 16.1–6
1 Cor. 16.19   Col. 4.15

8. Several times in this letter Paul said he was rejoicing or would rejoice. According to each of the following verses what was the reason for his joy:
   (a) 1.18   (b) 2.17   (c) 4.10
9. 'The Greek word translated "anxiety" or "care" sometimes means (i) "loving attention", and sometimes (ii) "worry" (p. 117). Which is the meaning in each of the following passages?
   (a) Matt. 10.19   (b) Matt. 13.22   (c) Luke 10.41
   (d) Luke 12.22   (e) Luke 21.34   (f) 1 Cor. 12.25
   (g) Phil. 2.20   (h) 1 Pet. 5.7a

DISCUSSION AND RESEARCH

10. 'These women have laboured side by side with me in the gospel' (v. 3). What opportunities are given to women in your Church to 'labour in the gospel'? How do they compare with the opportunities given to men? How do they compare with the opportunities given to women in other Churches in your area?
11. 'To what extent should the Church lead the rest of society, and to what extent should it accept the present conventions of society?' (p. 114).
    What is your own answer to this question?
12. In 4.4 Paul told his readers to 're joice in the Lord', and in 4.10 he said that he 'rejoiced greatly' although he was in prison and in danger of death. An evangelist in Cairo once said, 'The opposite of joy is not sorrow: it is sin.' What do you think he meant? Do you agree? Give your reasons.
13. 'Have no anxiety' (v. 6).
    (a) What did Paul tell the Philippians to do in order to get rid of their anxiety?
    (b) To what extent can Christians of today get rid of anxiety in the same way?
14. 'Do not make your plans in such a way that you trust God less' (p. 117). What does this mean in practice? Does it mean that a Church treasurer or the Matron of a home for orphans should pray rather than telling people of the need for money?
15. In vv 8 and 9 Paul pointed to the 'goodness' in people and told his readers to think about it and rejoice in it.
    (a) Think of people you know (whether they are Christians or not) in whom you see one or more of the sorts of 'goodness' which Paul listed in vv 8 and 9.
    (b) Thank God for them, and

(c) Ask yourself what you have learnt about God as a result of thinking about such people.

16. 'What you have learned . . . received and heard and seen . . . do!' (v. 9). What had the Philippians received and heard and seen in Paul that he now told them to *do*? To what extent is your own congregation doing those things?

4.10–23

Giving and Receiving

INTRODUCTION

When we read v. 10 of this section ('I rejoice that you have revived your concern for me') we may well ask, 'Why did Paul not thank the Philippians for their help more eagerly, and why did he wait until the end of his letter before thanking them at all?' We can find an answer to these questions if we agree that the following events took place before Paul wrote these verses (but in the case of (b) and (c) below, there is no evidence: they are suggestions only):

(a) The Philippians sent Paul a gift of money and a letter.

(b) Paul thanked them (in a letter which we have not got), but said that he did not need gifts in order to have joy.

(c) They replied, saying that they were disappointed at his letter and that he had been glad of gifts in the past.

(d) So Paul wrote this letter, including vv 10–20.

In these verses he was saying:

1. Your gift and your love did indeed make me joyful. You did more than anyone else! (vv 14–16).

2. But I must say clearly that I can be full of joy without receiving gifts. (vv 11–13).

3. Yet your gift was very important, especially the love with which you sent it. It was more than a gift to me, it was an offering to God. (vv 17–20).

4. Greetings and a prayer (vv 21–23).

The main idea in these verses is the link between 'giving' and 'receiving'. Paul had given his ministry to the Philippians and had received gifts from them. The Philippians had received Paul's ministry and had given him gifts. It was a partnership. Paul used the language of trading in vv 15 and 17 because it was language which they fully understood, and because there really had been an exchange of 'goods' between them.

But the Philippians had also given something to God (v. 18) and would receive something from God (v. 19). See note 3 on v. 15.

NOTES AND INTERPRETATION

I rejoice in the Lord greatly that now at length you have revived your concern for me (v. 10a):

I rejoice: Paul had been taken to Rome as a prisoner, after a voyage of great danger and discomfort. He was a prisoner for two years, and there were at first very few friends. And then 'at length' the gift and the letter came from the Philippians. Of course he rejoiced (but see note on 'rejoicing' in v. 4).

In the Lord: In this letter we find the following phrases: 'in Christ Jesus' (8 times), 'in the Lord' (8 times), 'in him' (twice), 'in the Lord Jesus' and 'in Christ'. What did Paul mean?

(a) It was his way of saying that a person lives as a Christian by being in fellowship with God who has shown Himself in Jesus Christ, now risen. If Paul was confident, it was because he was 'in the Lord' (1.14). If he was hopeful, it was because he was 'in the Lord Jesus' (2.19). If he could overcome adversity, it was because he was 'in him' (4.13).

Some readers have been surprised that Paul gave so little detailed instruction in this letter about Christian behaviour. We find the reason for this in the phrase 'in the Lord'. Paul meant 'live in the Lord and work out amongst yourselves how to live as a Christian in the world.' Compare 2.12.

(b) Although no one except Paul used these phrases about living 'in the Lord' or 'in Christ', we read of the same experience in other parts of the Bible. According to John, Jesus told his disciples, 'Abide in me, and I in you' (15.4). So Christians have Christ as the 'atmosphere' in which they live. As a fish is in the sea, and the sea is in the fish, as a bird is in the air and the air is in the bird, so a Christian is in Christ and Christ is in him.

An Indian Sikh read this phrase 'in the Lord' and said, 'I also have my "guru", my holy guide and counsellor, living in my own city. I live my life in him and he is the light for my darkness.' Christians believe that Jesus is far more than an invisible 'guru', but the words of this Sikh remind us that being 'in' the Lord means far more than following His laws.

(c) But being 'in Christ' does not mean enjoying a private and isolated fellowship with Him. Being 'in Christ' is at the same time being in His body, which is the Church: 'You are the body of Christ and individually members of it' (1 Cor. 12.27). Those who are 'in Christ' share that with all others who are 'in Him'.

(d) God does not force that fellowship upon us which comes from being 'in Christ'. We need to 'receive' it (See note on v. 15).

You had no opportunity (v. 10b): When Paul wrote 'at length (i.e. at last) you have revived your concern', he was not complaining about a delay. In order to make this clear, he added here that they had not previously had an opportunity. Either they had no messenger or they could not collect enough money to send. In 2 Corinthians 8.1, 2 we read that the Churches of Macedonia (which included the Philippians) were suffering 'severe affliction'.

The Greek word translated 'opportunity' means 'the right time', the opportunity which God has given and which may not come again. We find the same word in Jesus's question to the multitudes: 'Why do you not know how to interpret the present time?' (Luke 12.56). In 1 Corinthians 16.12 Paul said that Apollos would come 'when he has opportunity'.

I have learned, in whatever state I am, to be content (v. 11):

In whatever state: See five similar phrases: 'always' (v. 4), 'anything' (v. 6), 'everything' (v. 6), 'any and all circumstances' (v. 12), 'all things' (v. 13). Paul was saying that his state of mind depended on his fellowship with Christ, rather than on circumstances. There are, of course, circumstances in which no one could be 'content', e.g. when a person is being tortured, or has been mentally confused by drugs, or is suffering acute physical pain. But what Paul has said is no less true and no less important.

I have learned to be content: The Stoics and the Christians used the Greek word which is here translated 'content' or 'contented' (and often translated as meaning 'independent') with different meanings.

1. There were a great many Stoics in Tarsus, Paul's home town, and he understood their teachings well. They were taught to find 'contentment' by wanting fewer and fewer things, and by needing fewer and fewer other people, and by feeling pain and pleasure less and less. This they did by the strength of their own wills. So from childhood they did hardship exercises and disciplined themselves, severely controlling the amount that they ate, wearing only a few clothes in cold weather, and hiding any pain they felt.

2. It is clear that there was much in the life of a Stoic which Paul and other Christians could praise and imitate. Jesus taught that a 'man's life does not consist in the abundance of his possessions' (Luke 12.15). And Paul had said that he did not depend on circumstances in order to find joy (4.4). But while Stoics emphasized what they could *do without* through their own will-power, Paul emphasized what he could *do with* the help of Christ.

How was it that Paul could be so 'contented'?

(a) He knew that his own strength was not enough. He needed the strength which comes from being 'in Christ' (see note on 4.13).

(b) He believed that God had made human beings to depend on one another in many ways, not to be 'self-sufficient' (see note on 'partnership', v. 15).

(c) His work of caring for people left him no time to undertake 'hardship exercises'. But he accepted hardship if he met it while doing his work. This is the meaning of v. 11.

One student, after reading the above note, said, 'Most of us are neither like the Stoics nor like Paul. We neither stand on our own feet nor put our whole confidence in Christ. We fall in between.'

I know how to be abased, and I know how to abound . . . I have learned the secret of facing plenty and hunger (v. 12): In v. 11 Paul said that he could be 'content' in whatever state he was. In v. 12 he gave two examples:

(a) when things were going badly ('abased', 'hunger', 'want'),

(b) when things were going well ('abound', 'plenty', 'abundance').

He said that he had at last discovered how to keep in fellowship with Christ in either situation.

To be abased . . . facing hunger: Paul had been brought very low by ill-treatment and loneliness and want. 'We hunger and thirst, we are ill-clad and buffeted and homeless' (1 Cor. 4.11). 'Greater labours, far more imprisonments, with countless beatings and often near death' (2 Cor. 11.23, and see also vv 24–27). In a marvellous way Paul found himself able to say. 'when I am weak, then I am strong' (2 Cor. 12.10).

To abound . . . facing plenty: Paul had successes also. He could look back on all the congregations which existed because of his preaching. But he knew that success and prosperity could be a greater danger to his faith than 'abasement'. This is what writers in the New Testament (unlike writers in the Old Testament) taught. It follows the words of Jesus, 'How hard it will be for those who have riches to enter the kingdom of God!' (Mark 10.23). This is the reason why an old prayer which is still used in many parts of the Church contains the petition: 'In all times of our wealth, good Lord, deliver us.' Anything which leads people to depend less on God and on one another is dangerous.

Note: In writing, 'I have learnt the secret', Paul used a word which members of the Mystery Religions used (see note on 3.12). In those religions anyone could join in the usual worship, but only those who had 'learnt the secrets' (and took an oath not to tell anyone else) could take part in the more important events. Paul used this phrase when he was referring to any stage through which a Christian had to go and in which he needed faith and courage, e.g. baptism.

I can do all things in him who strengthens me (v. 13): Of course Paul was not saying that he could do everything. The six Greek words

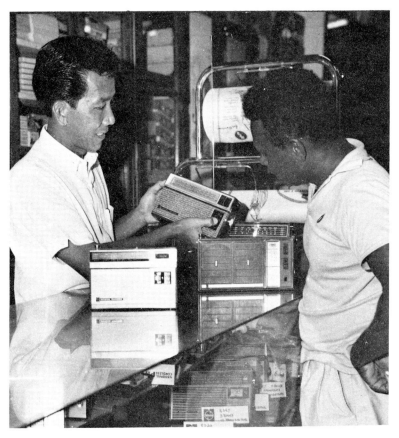

'No church entered into partnership with me in giving and receiving except you only' (4.15).

A customer in Rabaul, New Britain, is buying a transistor radio. What are he as the buyer of the radio, and the shopkeeper selling it, each giving and receiving? In what way is their 'giving' and 'receiving' different from the giving and receiving between Paul and the Philippians?

simply mean 'I am strong – everything in Him who strengthens me'. Other translations of this verse are: 'I have the strength to face all conditions by the power that Christ gives me' (GNB); 'I am ready for anything through the strength of the one who lives within me' (Phillips).

Oliver Cromwell, the seventeenth-century English revolutionary, found these words very comforting on two occasions in his life. First, when his eldest son died. Secondly, when he himself was dying he read this verse and said aloud, 'Paul, you have learnt this. But what shall I do, poor creature?' Then, after a while he said firmly, 'He that was Paul's Christ is my Christ too.'

For the words 'in him' see note on v. 10a, 'in the Lord'.

It was kind of you to share my trouble (v. 14):
Kind of you: The words mean 'you performed a beautiful deed'. The Philippians had not been sure if Paul had valued their gift, and so he assured them here that he certainly did value it.

Praise such as Paul gave them here is something which we all need, and which Jesus Himself often gave: 'Among those born of women none is greater than John' (Luke 7.28). Of the woman in the Pharisee's house He said, 'She has not ceased to kiss my feet . . . she loved much' (Luke 7.45–47). 'Daughter, your faith has made you well' (Luke 8.48). 'You have answered right' (Luke 10.28).

For most people it is not praise which makes them conceited. Conceited people are usually those whom no one has praised, and who are therefore trying to persuade others that they deserve to be praised.
Share: The Greek word is *koinonia* (see note on 1.5). Paul's readers could not remove his trouble, but they could share it. This sharing is one important way of expressing fellowship (*koinonia*) and it can be done with or without words, by letter or a visit or by a deed (as the Philippians did).

You Philippians yourselves know that in the beginning of the gospel, when I left Macedonia, no church entered into partnership with me in giving and receiving except you only (v. 15):
Beginning of the gospel: Paul was thinking of the beginning of his work in Philippi, when he first preached the gospel there (see Acts 16).
When I left Macedonia, that is to say, when Paul left Philippi and was on his way to Thessalonica (see Acts 17.1).
No church: i.e. no congregation except you had this sort of partnership, in which you gave me gifts and I gave you ministry.

(a) In the New Testament the word 'Church' always refers to people and never to a building. Christians did not use special buildings for worship or call them 'churches' until after AD 200. (In this Guide we use 'Church' to refer to people and 'church' to refer to a building.)

(b) The Greek word *'ecclesia'* (which we translate 'Church') means 'the assembly which is called out', i.e. called out by Jesus Christ from the world to do His work in the world. It is His body' (1 Cor. 12.27 and 28).

(c) *'Ecclesia'* was the word used for the congregation of the Israelites when they translated the Old Testament into Greek. This reminds us that the Christian Church is the transformed Twelve Tribes whom God called out to worship and serve Him as He called out Abraham.

(d) There is only one Church, *the* Church. Jesus spoke of 'my Church': 'On this rock I will build my church' (Matt. 16.18).

(e) But as groups of Christians began to meet together, each group in its own town or village, they began to say that there was *a* Church there (as Paul does in 4.15). 'When you assemble as a church' (1 Cor. 11.18). And they talked about 'the Churches' in the plural: 'All the churches of the Gentiles give thanks' (Romans 16.4). But those who used these phrases knew that what they called 'a Church' was in truth 'the Church' as people saw it in one place. A congregation 'represented' the whole Church. See Philemon 1.2: 'The church in your house'.

(f) Paul and other Christians of his time would not have understood the modern phrases, 'The Roman Catholic Church', 'The United Reformed Church'. He would have been as deeply distressed at these phrases as he was at the divisions in the congregation at Philippi. The phrases exist because God's Church is now divided, and because people have often forgotten that there is only one Church.

Entered into partnership with me: Once again we find the word *'koinonia'* (partnership).

In giving and receiving: As we have already noted (p. 125), these words sum up the truth which Paul most wanted to express in vv 10–23. There are three ways of understanding it:

1. *Giving and receiving go together:* They went together as Paul and the Philippians first met and later formed a partnership. Each gave to the other, each received from the other. See 1 Corinthians 3.8 where Paul wrote that an exchange of this sort was good and important in people's daily work: 'He who plants and he who waters are equal and each shall receive his wages.' In Romans 15.25–27 he explained how the congregations in Macedonia had received the gospel from Jerusalem, and now were sending contributions to the Church in Jerusalem: 'They have been pleased to make some contribution for the poor among the saints at Jerusalem . . . indeed they are in debt to them, for if the Gentiles have come to share in their spiritual blessings, they ought also to be of service to them in material blessings.'

In many countries today there is a 'partnership' or 'exchange' between one congregation and another. In a part of London where there is much unemployment and violence, the members of one congregation have become very courageous in helping people in their sufferings, and they are able to share this spirit of courage and caring with another congregation 20 miles away with which they are linked. This other congregation has more 'material blessings', and they share these with the Christians in London.

Another way in which an 'exchange' takes place is between the leader of a congregation and the members. There are a great many ways in which each gives to the other, although both leader and members often overlook the fact.

2. *Giving:* See note on v. 18b.

3. *Receiving:* It may seem from verses such as 11, 13, and 17 that Paul was rather unwilling to receive gifts of any sort. Probably there were times when he found it difficult. He was never willing to accept a gift from the Corinthians. 'Do we not have the right to our food and drink? . . . But I have made no use of these rights' (1 Cor. 9.4, 15). But he did receive the gift which Epaphroditus brought him (v. 18).

'Receiving' is not the same as 'taking'. In 'taking' we may enjoy asserting our independence (there is a proverb: 'stolen water is sweet', Prov. 9.17). But the person who receives is showing his dependence on the giver, and perhaps his gratitude to him. Indeed, some people need to learn how to receive gifts. A minister who once worked in the West Indies has told how he was visiting villages with some of his Church members on a very rainy day. He got so dirty and muddy that the others said, 'Stop. Let us clean you up.' But he wanted to do it himself and would not let them. After some time, he saw that they were distressed at his refusal (also he was not very successful at cleaning himself up!), so he said, 'Yes. Please help.' He calls this the time when he learnt the importance of receiving a gift.

Even in Thessalonica you sent me help (v. 16): This is another example of Paul's receiving help from the Philippians. As we have seen, after his first visit to Philippi, he went on to the seaport of Thessalonica. There it was the Philippians, not the people of Thessalonica, who gave him help – and gave him help twice.

Not that I seek the gift; but I seek the fruit which increases to your credit (v. 17): that is, 'which is to your advantage'.

Not that I seek: i.e. I am not anxiously waiting for a gift.

I seek the fruit: The word here translated 'fruit' means the 'interest' or 'profit' which people can get when they invest their money or put it into a bank. The 'nobleman' in Jesus's parable (Luke 19.12–24) told his servants to 'trade' with his money till he returned, i.e. to see that it brought an 'increase to his credit'. So Paul was saying: 'I believe that giving that gift will bring you even more advantages than it has brought me. You are now open to many blessings from God.' (He repeated this in v. 19.)

Paul was not saying that the Philippians had *earned* God's blessings by their goodness. That would have contradicted the clear teaching of such a passage as Romans 3.23, 24: 'Since all have sinned and fall short of the glory of God, they are justified by his grace as a gift.'

We can see what Paul meant by looking at 1 Corinthians 9.6–11 (e.g. 'who plants a vineyard without eating any of its fruit?' v. 7). A person who behaves generously becomes open to others and to God. Therefore he is open to receive greater gifts from others and from God. than before.

A widow who was very lonely was asked if she would allow the village school to use a room in her house. She was a shy person and did not want to do this. But because the school was in great need, she allowed them to use it. The result was that she made friends of all the children's parents and she became much less lonely.

This is also true concerning the way nations treat each other. Recently Gro Harlem Brundtland and a group of experts from many countries produced a report on 'Our Common Future'. They showed that rich countries need to reduce poverty in the world, not only to help the poor but in order to prevent the destruction of the world's environment. Some richer countries have asked 'Why should we care?' Mrs Brundtland's reply was 'Because if you care you will enable other countries and future generations to meet their needs, and at the same time to meet your own needs.' God has made the world one world.

I have received full payment, and more (v. 18a): i.e. 'If there was a debt which you owed me, then I tell you that it has been more than fully paid' (NEB: 'Here I give you my receipt for everything').

This may seem an unfriendly way in which to write to friends. But it is likely that Paul was doing nothing more than continuing the language of trading, which we noticed in vv 15 and 17. His readers probably understood it in that way.

I am filled, having received from Epaphroditus the gifts you sent, a fragrant offering, a sacrifice acceptable and pleasing to God (v. 18b): In this verse Paul was again making it clear that he was grateful for the Philippians' gifts. But he added that, in sending him a gift, they were also making an offering to God. 'Fragrant' or 'sweet-smelling' offering is a phrase which Old Testament writers had used for a sacrifice which worshippers believed to be 'acceptable and pleasing' to God. Perhaps in very early times they believed that the actual smell pleased God, and prevented Him from being angry (see Gen. 8.21). Later they knew that God is 'Spirit', but they continued to use the same phrase. We read in Ephesians 5.2 that when Jesus 'gave himself up for us' it was 'a fragrant offering and sacrifice to God'. See also Exodus 29.18.

In the same way, when present-day Christians, at a cost to themselves, make offerings to people in need, they are making an offering to God Himself 'As you did it to one of the least of these my brethren, you did it to me' (Matt. 25.40). They do it as a sort of response to God's own giving of Himself in Jesus Christ. Would Church members be likely to give more generously if they were given this teaching more clearly?

My God will supply every need of yours according to his riches in glory in Christ Jesus (v. 19): This verse is like a box of books which you cannot read till they have been unpacked. Paul was so overflowing with gratitude to God and with hope for his readers that he did not stop to write down his thoughts carefully. The thoughts are crowded together in one short sentence.

The best way to interpret this sentence is probably: 'My God will generously ("according to his riches") supply every need of yours as you live in Christ ("in Christ Jesus") thus showing forth His Glory ("in glory").'

We may picture a father in Philippi hearing someone reading this out. Perhaps a gang of youths has just violently attacked his young son because of his connection with the Christian Church, and the need of the family is very great. When the verse is read out: 'God *will* supply . . .', he is encouraged and goes home with new confidence. Compare 4.7 'The peace of God . . . *will* keep your hearts and minds'; and 2 Corinthians 9.10: 'He who supplies seed to the sower and bread for food *will* supply and multiply your resources.'

Note that some people think that 'glory' refers to the glory which Christ will show forth at His 'Coming', and they translate the last seven words as 'when you enter into His coming glory' (see note (f) on p. 135).

My God: See note on 1.3.

Riches: See Romans 2.4 for another verse where Paul wrote of God's 'riches': 'The riches of his kindness and forbearance and patience.'

Glory: This is one of the great Bible words.

(a) Usually it means the showing forth of God's being and power. 'The heavens are telling the glory of God' (Ps. 19.1).

(b) In the New Testament it is usually the 'showing forth of God's being in Jesus Christ'. John 1.14: 'we have beheld his glory, glory as of the only Son from the Father.'

(c) In the Fourth Gospel 'glory' sometimes means the showing forth of God's being when Jesus gave Himself to die for mankind. In John 17.1 are words spoken just before He died, e.g. 'Father, the hour has come; glorify thy Son.'

(d) 'Giving glory to God' (as in v. 20 of this chapter) means acknowledging His being and His power. See also Revelation 19.7: 'Let us rejoice . . . and give Him the glory.'

(e) Human beings can partially share in God's being and power, and therefore can share in God's glory. John 17.22: 'Thy glory which thou has given me I have given to them'; 'Our glorification' (1 Cor. 2.7).

(f) There is glory which human beings cannot share until the 'Coming'. Romans 8.18: 'The sufferings of this present time are not worth comparing with the glory that is to be revealed to us.'

(g) We should also note that in Old Testament times 'glory' often meant 'weight', 'status', 'wealth', beauty', 'shining-bright'. See Genesis 45.13, where Joseph said, 'Tell my father of all my glory in Egypt.'

Note: In some translations the Greek word for 'boasting' is also translated 'glorying'. But that is a different Greek word from the one used here (see note on 3.3).

Greet every saint in Christ Jesus (v. 21a): It seems to have been Paul's custom to write the last few verses of a letter himself, although he had dictated the rest of it. This seems likely from 1 Corinthians 16.21: 'I, Paul, write this greeting with my own hand.'

Every saint: For 'saint' see note on 1.1. On this occasion Paul greeted all the congregation together. He did not send messages to individuals, as he did for example in Colossians 4.15. Probably this was in order to avoid jealousy and division in the Church.

In Christ Jesus: See note on 4.10. This means, 'Greet all the saints because we are all in Christ Jesus.'

The brethren who are with me greet you (v. 21b):

Brethren: See note on 1.12.

Who are with me: It is possible that Paul wrote this part of the letter some time after he wrote 2.21. In 2.21 he had said that the people who were with him were not working happily with him. They 'all looked after their own interests, not those of Jesus Christ.' But now they joined with Paul in sending greetings. Unhelpful Christians *can* become helpful Christians! Perhaps this is what had happened among the Philippians.

All the saints greet you, especially those of Caesar's household (v. 22): It was a remarkable event which Paul mentioned here, and one for which he was rejoicing as he wrote this. There in Rome (or it may have been Ephesus, see pp 28, 29), amongst the officials of the great Roman Empire, were people coming secretly to Paul in their free time, to talk and pray and sing, and eat together. They came secretly because they could have been dismissed or punished in other ways if they had been discovered. It was known that Christians served a King and called Him the 'King of Kings': 'These men have turned the world upside down . . . saying that there is another king, Jesus' (Acts 17.6, 7); 'The blessed and only Sovereign, the King of kings' (1 Tim. 6.15). So it was not surprising if they were thought to be disloyal to the Emperor.

Who were these people 'of Caesar's household'? They were not the Emperor's own family, but officials who served the Roman Empire. There were palace officials, secretaries, treasurers, and body-guards. Some were slaves, others free citizens; some were Romans, but there were also Greeks, Syrians, Egyptians, and others. It was from this 'household' that the 'saints' came.

Probably they could well understand the position in which the Philippians were placed, because they too were a tiny minority living among people who were hostile to Christians. We do not know if they knew of Jesus's words, 'Blessed are you when men revile you . . . on my account. Rejoice and be glad, for your reward is great in heaven' (Matt. 5.11, 12).

The grace of the Lord Jesus Christ be with your spirit (v. 23): In Church services today Christians sometimes end with this sentence, but often forget what it means because it has become so familiar. When Paul first wrote it to the Philippians, he probably meant this, 'I will end my letter with a prayer: may God who in Jesus Christ loves us and treats us so much more generously than we deserve (in His "grace") live in you all ("with your spirit").' See notes on 'grace' (1.2 and 29), 'spirit' (3.3).

STUDY SUGGESTIONS

WORDS

1. 'Church' (v. 15). In each of the following sentences the writer used the word 'church' in a different way. Re-write them so as to show clearly what 'church' means in each case.
   (a) Our church leaks.
   (b) The church in Britain disagrees with the State concerning the present Nationality Bill.
   (c) My church has no minister at present.
   (d) Most Christians in the Philippines belong to the Roman Catholic church.
   (e) The church's one foundation
       Is Jesus Christ her Lord.
2. With which of the meanings in Q.1 did Paul use the word 'church' in v. 15?

CONTENT

3. 'In the Lord' (v. 10).
   (a) What did Paul mean by this phrase?
   (b) Find as many instances as you can of other phrases that Paul used in this letter to describe the experience of being 'in the Lord'.

4. In what ways did Paul's 'contentment' (v. 11) differ from the contentment of the Stoics?
5. 'It was kind of you to share my trouble' (v. 14). To what 'trouble' was Paul referring when he praised the Philippians in this way?
6. What did Paul mean by 'fruit which increases to your credit' (v. 17)?
7. (a) Who were 'those of Caesar's household' (v. 22)?
   (b) Why was it remarkable that they sent greetings to the Philippians?

BIBLE

8. Paul, like Jesus, was grateful for help he received from others (see p. 133, note on v. 18b). What was Jesus willing and glad to receive according to each of the following passages?
   (a) Luke 5.3 (b) Luke 7.37–38 (c) Luke 10.38–42
   (d) Luke 14.1 (e) John 4.6, 7 (f) John 6.11
9. 'Glory: this is one of the great Bible words' (p. 134). What is meant by the word 'glory' (v. 19) in each of the following passages?
   (a) Ps. 45.3 (b) John 2.11 (c) John 12.27, 28 (d) Gal. 1.5
   (e) 2 Thess. 2.14
10. In what ways do the following verses (a) resemble, (b) differ from Phil. 4.21a? 1 Cor. 16.21 Gal. 6.11 Col. 4.18 2 Thess. 3.17

DISCUSSION AND RESEARCH

11. 'I have learned to be content' (v. 11). Describe from your own experience some of the ways in which a Christian can 'learn' to be content. Do you agree with the student's statement on p. 128, that most Christians fall in between the Stoics and Paul, in their ability to be content? Give reasons for your answer.
12. 'Facing hunger . . . facing plenty' (see v. 12). Which do you think is the greater danger to a person's faith, to be very rich or to be very poor? Give your reasons.
13. In what ways, if any, does the teaching of your own Church help people to remember that 'there is only one Church'?
14. After hearing a sermon based on the teaching that 'It is more blessed to give than to receive', a woman said: 'But no one can give unless someone else, by receiving, gives them the opportunity to give. Surely the "receiver" and the "giver" are equally "blessed"!' What is your opinion?
15. 'Partnership . . . in giving and receiving' (v. 15). What are some of the ways in which a minister and his congregation can enter into a partnership by giving to each other?
16. 'Praise . . . is something we all need' (p. 130).
   (a) For what did Paul praise the Philippians?
   (b) Why is it important to praise others?
   (c) What is the difference between praise and flattery?

List of Special Word Studies

References are to the verse in Philippians where each word is chiefly discussed. Page references to these studies are given in the Index in bold type.

Key to Study Suggestions

1.1 and 2

3. See p. 1, lines 2–4.

4. (a) See p. 5, numbered para. 4.
   (b) See p. 5, numbered para. 1.

5. See p. 5, lines 15–5 from foot.

6. See p. 7, lines 13–16.

7. See p. 4, numbered para. 1, line 2.

8. (a) A place set apart.
   (b) The Sabbath day.
   (c) Faithful Jews.
   (d) Christians.
   (e) Christians in Philippi.
   (f) Writings.

1.3–8

1. (a) Sharing, communion, acceptance, fellowship, participation.
   (b) See p. 12, numbered paras 1 and 2.

2. (a) My.   (b) See p. 11, line 13.

3. See vv 5 and 7.

4. (a) Four.   (b) See p. 11, line 37.

5. V. 3: He did not forget them, but kept in touch.
   Vv 5 and 6: (a) They were partners.   (b) Paul had confidence in them.
   V. 7: Paul loved them greatly.

6. See p. 15, lines 24–27.

7. (a) (ii)   (b) (iii)   (c) (ii)   (d) (iii)   (e) (ii)   (f) (i)

8. (a) It must first be preached to the Gentiles.
   (b) It is the power of God for salvation.
   (c) Not everyone has listened to it.
   (d) Preaching it is necessary, but not a thing to boast about.
   (e) His hearers heard it. In it they stand. . . . By it they were saved.

9. See p. 16, 21–25.

10. (a) That day.
    (b) The day of our Lord Jesus Christ.
    (c) The day of redemption.
    (d) The day of the Lord.
    (e) That day.
    (f) The day of the Lord.

11. (a) See p. 12, numbered para. 2.
    (c) See p. 13, numbered para. 6.

1.9–11

1. See p. 20, para. (b).

2. (b) Patient, caring, long-suffering, forgiving, sustaining.

3. Increase, augment, be abundant, grow.

4. See p. 20, note on v. 9b.

5. See pp 19 and 20, paras (a) and (b).

6. See p. 22, note on v. 10.

7. See p. 22, note on v. 11.

8. (a) (i) Peter.   (ii) That his faith should remain firm.
   (b) (i) Those who crucified Him.   (ii) That they should be forgiven.
   (c) (i) Philip and other disciples.
       (ii) That they should receive the Holy Spirit.
   (d) (i) His disciples.
       (ii) That God would keep them safe and that they might be united.
   (e) (i) Those whom the disciples helped to believe.
       (ii) That they should be united.

10. (a) See p. 21, note on v. 9c.

12. See p. 21, lines 20–23.

1.12–18

1. *Teaching*: guiding, instructing, training, explaining.
   Preaching: declaring, announcing, witnessing, challenging.

3. See p. 25, last para.

4. See p. 30, top para.

5. See p. 26, (d).

6. (a) (i) Jesus.   (ii) Repent: the kingdom of heaven is at hand.
   (b) (i) Disciples.   (ii) The resurrection.
   (c) (i) Philip.   (ii) Good news about Jesus.
   (d) (i) Paul.   (ii) Jesus and the resurrection.
   (e) (i) Paul.   (ii) Christ crucified.

7. (a) Imprisonment.   (b) Separation from friends.
   (c) Hearing bad news from Philippi.
   (d) Knowing that they might soon kill him.
   (e) Worrying about Epaphroditus's illness.
   (f) Seeing the un-Christ-like behaviour of some Christians.
   (g) Being abased, hungry, and in want.

1.19–26

1. (a), (b), (d), (e) See note on v. 19c.

2. (a) See p. 33, note on v. 20.

3. See pp 32 and 33, notes on v. 19a and 19b.

4. See p. 33, note on v. 19c.

5. (a) See p. 36, notes (a) to (f) on v. 21b.
   (b) See p. 36, note on v. 21b, lines 4, 9, 10.
   (c) See p. 36, note on v. 21b, lines 4–6.

6. They were dragged into the market place, accused of breaking the law, had their clothes torn off them, were beaten, put in prison, and had their feet put in the stocks.

7. (a) No remembrance or prayer is possible.
   (b) No prayer, no hope.
   (c) It is a completion of life.
   (d) It cannot separate us from the love of God.
   (e) It means being with Christ.
   (f) Christ has abolished its terror.
   (g) It means being with the Lord and being at rest.

8. (a) (i).   (b) (ii).   (c) (iii).   (d) (iii).   (e) (i).

1.27–30

2. Sign, warning, forecast, hint.

4. (a) See p. 41, paras 1 and 2, and also p. 2 lines 3–13.
   (b) See p. 41, line 9, and p. 42, lines 10–13.

5. So that people should have confidence in God through hearing the gospel.

6. See p. 45, lines 4–10.

7. (i) See p. 41, last para.
   (ii) In (a), (c), (d), (e) 'worthy' means the same as in Phil. 1.27. In (b), (f), (g) it means 'good enough'.

2.1–4

1. (a) *Support*; console, cheer, comfort, sustain.
       Appeal: urge, incite, stir up, persuade.
   (b) (i) Support   (ii) Appeal.

2. 'In one spirit'. 'With one mind'. 'Side by side'. 'Of the same mind'. 'In full accord'. 'Of one mind'.

3. (a) See p. 50, lines 5, 6.
   (b) See p. 49, note on v. 2.

4. Paul cared deeply about their unity. It 'completed' his joy. Their relationship was close.

5. See p. 47, lines 1, 2.
   (a) (i).   (b) (ii).   (c) (ii).   (d) (ii).   (e) (i).

2.5–11

1. Character, nature, power, authority, appointment.

3. How can we have unity?

4. (a) See p. 54, paras (a) and (b)

6. See p. 55, last two paras.

141

7. (a) He was God's servant (Isa. 52.13 and Matt. 12.18) because He was obedient to God.

(b) He bore the sufferings of the world (Isa. 53.4) and did not come to be served but to serve (Matt. 20.28).

8. (i) (a) Like Phil. 2.7a shows Jesus as a servant.

(b) and (c) Like Phil. 2.7a these verses show that Jesus was a real human being.

9. (a) The man who sat in the place of honour was humbled. The one who sat in the lowest place was exalted.

(b) The Pharisee was humbled, the tax-collector was exalted.

(c) Paul was humbled, and Paul was exalted.

2.12–18

1. (a) See p. 69, middle para.

(b) Those who fail to acknowledge God's authority.

2. (a) See p. 66, lines 11–3 from foot.

(b) Worry, terror, panic, mistrust, alarm.

3. See p. 70, line 20.

4. See p. 63, note on v. 12a, lines 1–6.

5. See p. 64, line 14.

6. (a) See p. 67, last 10 lines; p. 68, line 8; p. 69, last 4 lines.

(b) See p. 69, 11 lines from foot.

7. Recognizing the gifts which God had given him, and using them, and thanking God for them.

8. See p. 71, lines 5–7.

9. (a) v. 15. (b) v. 15. (c) v. 16. (d) v. 18. (e) v. 17.

11. See p. 66, lines 5–10.

2.19–30

1. (a) Worried.

(b) No. Caring. Interested in.

2. See p. 77, note on v. 29a, lines 6–9.

3. See p. 73. Introduction.

4. See p. 74, paras (a), (b), (c), (d).

5. See p. 73, last 2 lines, and p, 74, lines 1–8.

6. See p. 76, last 2 lines.

7. See p. 76, lines 1–4.

8. (a) (i). (b) (iii). (c) (ii). (d) (i). (e) (ii). (f) (iii). (g) (iii).

9. (a) By seeing that God keeps covenant, that He is faithful.

(b) By seeing that God supports the weak.

(c) By having his wounds bound up.

(d) By receiving his sight.

(e) By being born again into a living hope.

3.1–11

1. See p. 86, note on 'Righteousness'.
2. See p. 88, lines 14–25.
3. An invisible force. The Holy Spirit of God.
4. (b) See p. 90, note on 'Faith'.
5. See p. 81, last 10 lines, and p. 82, lines 1–15.
6. See p. 81, lines 20–30.
7. See p. 83, lines 13–26.
8. See p. 84, last 12 lines.
9. (a) See p. 85, last 11 lines, and p. 86, lines 1–10.
   (b) See p. 88, last 8 lines.
10. See p. 92, lines 22–26, and last 7 lines.
11. (i) (a) Spiritual.   (b) Physical.   (c) Spiritual.
    (d) Physical.   (e) Spiritual.
12. (a) By carrying the man onto the top of the roof (Mark 2.3–5).
    (b) By keeping on calling out (Mark 10.46–52.).
    (c) By believing that Jesus could heal his servant (Luke 7.2–9).
    (d) By trusting in what Christ had done rather than in their own achievements (Gal. 2.14–16).
    (e) By going out without knowing where God was leading him (Heb. 11.8).

3.12–16

1. (a) See p. 96, last 8 lines, and p. 97, lines 1–12.
   (b) Mature.
2. See p. 96, Introduction.
3. (a) See p. 99, lines 5–7.
4. (a) running and boxing   (b) running   (c) running
   (d) boxing and running   (e) running.
5. (a) It comes through His Son.
   (b) It comes through other people.
   (c) It comes to sinners.
   (d) He calls some people to positions of authority.
   (e) It is a call to follow Jesus.
   (f) It comes today, now.
7. See p. 97, note on v. 13b.

3.17—4.1

1. See p. 108, note on 'A saviour'.
3. (a) See p. 109, numbered paras 2 and 3.
   (b) See p. 109, lines 6–12, and numbered para. 4.
4. See p. 110, 'love and long for'.

5. (a) See 2.15; 3.2; 3.18.
   (b) See p. 110, 'subject all things'.
6. (a) (i) Wander (NEB).
   (b) (i) Go on your way, journey (NEB); Live (GNB).
   (c) (i) Guided by (NEB); Walk (GNB).
   (d) (i) Followed (NEB, GNB).
   (e) (i) Live (NEB); Walk (GNB).
   (f) (i) Live (NEB, GNB).
7. V. 20.
8. (a) Place where God is.
   (b) God. (c) God.
   (d) Sky *or* Place where God is.
   (e) Sky *or* Place where God is.
   (f) Sky. (g) God. (h) Sky.

4.2–9

1. (a) See p. 116, lines 10–22.
   (b) Forgiving, considerate, generous, gentle, meek, merciful.
2. See p. 113, note on 'Agree in the Lord'.
4. See p. 114, 8 lines from end.
5. See p. 120, last 13 lines, and p. 121, lines 1–25.
6. See p. 118, line 10 to end of page, and p. 120, lines 21–27.
7. That women often held leading positions, especially among Christians.
8. (a) See p. 30, lines 6 and 7.
   (b) See p. 71, numbered para. 4, lines 1–8.
   (c) See p. 126, note on v. 18.
9. (a) (ii) (b) (ii) (c) (ii) (d) (ii) (e) (ii) (f) (i) (g) (i) (h) (ii)

4.10–23

1. (a) Our church building leaks.
   (b) The Christians in Britain disagree with the State. . . .
   (c) My congregation has no minister at present.
   (d) Most of the Christians in the Philippines belong to the Roman Catholic branch of the Church.
   (e) The Church's one foundation
       Is Jesus Christ her Lord.
2. (c) .
3. (a) See p. 126, note on 'in the Lord'.
   (b) See p. 126, lines 14, 15.
4. See p. 128, lines 1–7.
5. Being in prison.
6. See p. 133, lines 1–7.

7. (a) See p. 136, lines 1–6.
   (b) See p. 135, last para.
8. (a) Simon's boat.
   (b) The woman's ointment and her tears.
   (c) Hospitality from Mary and Martha.
   (d) Dinner from the Pharisee.
   (e) Water from the woman.
   (f) Loaves and fish from the boy.
9. (a) Status, shining bright.
   (b) Showing forth God's being in Jesus.
   (c) Showing forth God's being by giving Himself to die.
   (d) Acknowledging God's being and His power.
   (e) Humans partially sharing in God's being and His power.
10. (a) They are all greetings.
    (b) All except Phil. 4.21a say 'with my own hand'.
16. See p. 130, lines 14–25.

Index

This Index does not include the name of Jesus Christ, nor the names of Paul or the Philippians, because these names appear on almost every page of the Guide. Bold type indicates the pages where a word or theme is studied in detail (see also the List of Special Word Studies, p. 138).